# WHAT OTHERS ARE SAYING ABOUT THIS BOOK:

"*RV Traveling Tales* is the perfect companion for the adventurous writer. Within its pages you will find the intimate lives of women who have experienced the essence of life and nature. These women followed their heart as the writing-life journey took them to the open road."

> **Sheri' McConnell**, founder and president, National Association of Women Writers (NAWW) www.naww.org

"Captivating capsules of RV truths, travel and trivia, told by women who love the choices and challenges of RV life."

> **Janet Groene**, author of *Living Aboard Your RV, Cooking Aboard Your RV, Great Eastern RV Trips*, and many other travel books. www.gordonandjanetgroene.com

"More Americans than ever are swapping brick and mortar for the freedom and adventure of life on the roll. This collection of essays comes straight from the hearts of women who've actually lived the vagabond dream. A must-read for anyone who is contemplating the 'full-timing' lifestyle, *RV Traveling Tales* is entertaining, instructive and inspiring."

> **Mark C. Sedenquist**, editor of www.RoadTripAmerica.com

"The enlightening and heartwarming stories in *RV Traveling Tales* are easy to read and this book would be invaluable for any woman considering the open road. I cried, sighed and laughed and was amazed at some of the stories."

> **Barb Hofmeister**, co-author of *An Alternative Lifestyle* & *Movin'On*, www.movinon.net.

"A very personal collection of stories told by women who RV . . . about the challenges, joys, unexpected encounters, and friendships they find on the road, some while traveling with partners, others while traveling solo."

> **Dee Johnson**, RVing Women, www.rvingwomen.org

"After reading *RV Traveling Tales: Women's Journeys on the Open Road*, I felt warmed to the core, as if I'd just spent a long afternoon over coffee or an evening around a campfire sharing heartfelt feelings, growth experiences, and magical adventures with treasured friends. Most inspiring!"

**Sasha Sterling**, Editor, *RV Consumer Group*, www.rv.org

"*RV Traveling Tales: Women's Journeys on the Open Road* is a stimulating collection of essays describing experiences associated with the RV lifestyle. Whether from a full-time or short-term perspective, the joys and pitfalls of a mobile existence are described with humor and insight. From a teenager who has traveled nearly all of her young life to an adult daughter trying to keep up with the antics of her 83-year-old RVing mother and new stepfather, these are real women who are eager to find out what's around every bend in the road."

**Maxye Henry**, *MotorHome* and *Motorhome America Journal*

"As a woman who traveled full-time for many years, but who is currently grounded, *RV Traveling Tales: Women's Journeys On The Open Road*, allowed me to relive the adventure, the camaraderie, and magic that the RV lifestyle has to offer. The touching and greatly varied stories shared by my RVing sisters on the pages of this book made my pulse quicken and my feet itch with wanderlust!"

**Cathie Carr**, CEO, Escapees RV Club, www.escapees.com

"I love the stories. It's a great read. I'm motivated to get out there and get going!"

**Debbie Robus**, publisher *Workamper News*, www.workamper.com

# RV TRAVELING TALES

# WOMEN'S JOURNEYS ON THE OPEN ROAD

EDITED BY JAIMIE HALL AND ALICE ZYETZ

Grateful acknowledgment is made for the use of the following material:
- "A Cup of Tea and Nothing" by Megan Edwards, excerpted from *Roads From the Ashes,* © 1999 by Megan Edwards.
- "A Fine Bit of Madness" and "Agony of De-Feet" by Joei Carlton Hossack © 2001, reprinted by permission of the author.
- "The Mighty Yukon River" by Sharlene Minshall, condensed from a story in the 2002 edition of *RVing Alaska and Canada,* © 2002 with permission from the author.
- "House on Francis Mountain" by Kay Peterson, condensed from original printed in *Rainbow Chasers* © 1980 reprinted by permission of the author.
- "Why We Like Full-Timing" and "Eating Our Way Across the U.S.A." by Donia Steele, excerpted from *Steeles on Wheels* © 2002 by Donia and Mark Steele.

In order to protect privacy, some names have been changed.

Cover Design by Robert Aulicino
Cover photo of Alaska Highway by Bill Hall
Page design by Cheshire Dave Beckerman
Isadora font from Adobe; AGaramond Regular Small Caps from www.myfonts.com
Proofreading, 2nd printing: Adrienne Kristine

Publisher's Cataloging-in-Publication Data
(Provided by Quality Books, Inc.)

RV traveling tales : women's journeys on the open road /
   edited by Jaimie Hall and Alice Zyetz.
      p. cm.
   Includes index.
   LCCN 2002114592
   ISBN 0-9716777-2-7/978-0-9716777-2-2

   1. Recreational vehicle living. 2. Women travelers—
Anecdotes. I. Hall, Jaimie. II. Zyetz, Alice.

TX1110.R88 2003              796.7'9'082
                      QBI02-200832

FOR ALL OUR WOMEN CONTRIBUTORS—AND TO OTHER WOMEN WITH STORIES TO TELL. MAY THEY FIND THEIR VOICE, SHARE THEIR STORIES, AND ENRICH ALL OUR LIVES.

# Acknowledgements

Without our authors, there would be no book. We appreciate the fifty women who have generously shared their special stories with us, painting the RV life with its beauty, friendships, quirks, laughter, tears, and some very ordinary routines.

A special thank you to Cheshire Dave Beckerman for his graphic conception of what the stories should look like and for choosing the beautiful font (Isadora) for the titles. Isadora dances across the pages. And thank you to Robert Aulicino, who designed our brilliant cover. Bill Hall's photo of the Alaska Highway on the cover captures the beauty and the lure of the open road.

Many people answered our call for help in selecting the title and description of the book. We thank them all. Special thanks go to five people. Stephanie Bernhagen read the manuscript, offering excellent suggestions; she has been a supporter from the very beginning of the process. We were fortunate to have the benefit of two fine editors, Maxye Henry and Debbie Robus, whose suggestions were very useful in our final stages. Janice Lasko answered urgent questions about all aspects of producing the book. Adrienne Kristine proofed the manuscript for the second printing; we appreciate her sharp eye.

Thank you again to our respective husbands, Bill Hall and Chuck Zyetz, for their advice and especially their patience. Both men have lived through not one but two books each. They deserve the highest medals of honor our country can bestow.

And we must express our appreciation to each other. We have been in the same room for only twelve days during this 18-month process. The rest of the time we have communicated by e-mail, telephone, and postal service. We are still dear friends.

# Table of Contents

**THE LAST WORD**

HTTP://WWW.RVTRAVELINGTALES.COM

# Foreword

## by
## Steve Zikman

*co-author of Chicken Soup for the Traveler's Soul*

Last year, I started planning a 47-city cross-country "See America 2002" RV tour to promote *Chicken Soup for the Traveler's Soul*. Now, please understand that I had never even been *in* an RV before, so this was going to be a whole new adventure for me.

I did know that with the hectic schedule of a tour, I would need someone to drive the 37-foot Coachmen motorhome. Fortunately, I had met Janice Lasko, editor of the *Escapees* magazine, who placed a short blurb in the publication inviting members to apply for the position.

I received over fifty replies, whittled that number down to a shortlist and ended up interviewing the prospective drivers. One husband and wife team was Cathy and Tony Cirocco.

Cathy and Tony have been full-time RVers for more than eight years and, from the moment we got together, we hit it off. We seemed to have a natural ease with one another and, *most* importantly, we enjoyed good food and copious amounts of laughter — the perfect ingredients for a three and a half month excursion across America.

We met up in New York City at the end of April and a couple of days later, we headed upstate to get "the Rig." By that point, I had learned about RV life enough to call it "the Rig," but I was still, in fact, an RV virgin — I had yet to step foot in one. Arriving at the Campers' Barn in Kingston, New York, we couldn't miss the rig if we tried — it was bright yellow with a 12-foot chicken on its side. Tony and Cathy quickly dubbed it "the big, yellow chicken."

Our inspection complete, Tony took his place in the driver's seat. It was a cold, rainy day but I had the biggest smile across my face. I sat at the dinette table and couldn't wait to hit the open road.

One turn of the key and the diesel engine kicked in. Tony shifted into gear and, slowly, we made our way out of the parking lot and onto the pavement. We were on the road . . . in an RV!

I screeched with joy. Tony and Cathy wondered what all the fuss was about. They too were excited to begin the trip, but my joy was about much more than that. It was the joy of feeling the power *and* comfort of being in the rig, the thrill of being in a home—on wheels. I had traveled through more than fifty countries on six continents but never like this.

For the first couple of weeks, we were on a whirlwind schedule through the Northeast. In the space of a few days and hundreds of miles, we learned to work together and have a whole lot of fun.

As we headed across the Midwest, our camaraderie deepened as we found a natural and comfortable routine. Of course, we had our differences but we talked them out and worked them through, as RVers do. Committed to the journey, we were committed to each other.

At times, we'd be apart for a few days and then hook up again—at a hotel in Des Moines, in a campground near the Grand Canyon, or on the beach in Monterey. It was a wonderful feeling to spot the "big, yellow chicken," open the door, and feel at home with my newfound friends. Eagerly, we'd catch up, share a meal, and continue as if we'd never been away.

I learned that RVing is about people, places, and adventure. I saw firsthand that RV life is ripe with stories of laughter, caring, and most especially, friendship.

This splendid collection is about all of that and more. *RV Traveling Tales: Women's Journeys on the Open Road* will fan your wanderlust and serve as a rich oasis for your roving soul. It is a magnificent tribute to its many contributors, celebrating a life of passion filled with an insatiable curiosity for what lies around the next bend.

As for Cathy and Tony, after more than 8000 miles, we celebrated the end of one phase of our friendship and looked forward to our next adventure. We gave each other a great big hug (I've also learned that RVers love to hug) and said our farewells . . . until the next time, somewhere on the great open road.

Writer Tim Cahill must have had RVers in mind when he wrote, "A journey is best measured in friends rather than miles."

# Introduction

In the fall of 1994, we (Alice and Jaimie) were among a group of five women who gathered in Jaimie's RV to do writing practice led by Alice. That meeting is described in our first piece, "A Day of the Heart," by Betty Prange. This was the first of many such sessions that continue today, with different women writers, in different locations. That day neither of us had an inkling that we would one day team up to edit this anthology or that all five original participants in the writing group would be represented in its pages. The book is also influenced by another gathering held that same weekend, as told by DeAnna White, in her piece, "Women's Friendships." Since that Sunday, eight years ago, we have appreciated the importance of communication with other women in our RV travels.

As we put together this book, our dream was threefold. First was to give voice to RV women writers who have stories to tell. Some of our authors have been published; many have not. Second was to offer a companion to women on the road for those times when they feel isolated and hunger for women friends. And third was to give a peek into the RV lifestyle as experienced by women. For women considering or investigating the RV lifestyle, these stories provide a glimpse of what it is like.

Many RVers' relatives and friends think that full-time RVing is like an extended vacation. In fact, real life goes on—joys, illness, death, and mundane tasks like doing the laundry and shopping for groceries. Change does not stop even if the setting does. RVing enables our women to taste a sampler plate of life in different communities. It enables and sometimes forces growth. Opportunities for new adventures and giving back arise.

These stories evoke pictures of beautiful places, frustration and triumphs, laughter and tears. They present both the everyday and the special gifts of traveling. We hope you enjoy them as much as we have in putting them together for you.

Alice and Jaimie

P.S. To help with RV terminology used in the stories, we have included a glossary of terms on page 216.

# What is Full-Timing?

Full-time RVers live 365 days a year in their rig. This lifestyle opens up special opportunities. In the following stories, our writers share experiences that full-time RVing brings.

*Sometimes a simple event has far-reaching consequences. So it was*
*for Betty on a day in an RV in Pena Blanca. Not only did*
*Betty find women friends, but she also discovered the*
*richness of the RV lifestyle. This day was*
*also the genesis of this book.*

# A Day of the Heart

Betty Prange

THE WEAK LATE NOVEMBER SUN SHONE INTO PENA BLANCA canyon, a narrow slice of desert landscape two miles from the Mexico-Arizona border. The few hours of direct sun were no match for the nighttime temperatures in the teens. But inside the Pace Arrow it didn't matter. Five of us sat circled, or as close a proximity to that shape as permitted by the oblong box in which we gathered. Each of us held a pad of paper and a pen.

At Alice's suggestion we had gathered for a writing exercise, based on Natalie Goldberg's book, *Writing Down the Bones*. "Just keep your hand moving. Don't edit, let your thoughts go," Alice said. "When you finish, we will read them aloud, but will not critique them."

The lead weight in my stomach sunk lower. On command I was supposed to write on a topic, not yet assigned, and then read it to four mere acquaintances. I could say I had to use the toilet and not return. But Alice, born teacher, moved quickly and enthusiastically.

"We will write for five minutes, starting with the words, 'I remember.'"

I do not have the foggiest recollection what I scribbled, but eight years later I remember what the others wrote and my reaction. Jaimie shared the recent final days of her mother's life. Tears flowed, a tissue box was passed. There was silence when she finished. How, I wondered, could we read anything after that, and how could this woman be so open?

I remember the rhythm of dialog in Alice's story. How did she capture utterances so clearly? How, in so few words, could she manifest the personalities of her family?

Judy's gentle voice evoked a description of her childhood bedroom. She didn't tell us its meaning; she let us feel it through her words.

DeAnna stretched her legs and read what she had written. It unfolded like her long, graceful limbs, enveloping us in her history just as I have learned her personality embraces and welcomes people into her world.

Who were these people and where did they learn to express themselves so beautifully? We ignored Alice's stricture about critiquing. We shared our awe and appreciation for what each had written.

In that beautiful, cold canyon, on that short November day, five women bonded. Close female friendships were lacking in my life before then. Those women gave trust and openness. They will always be special to me. But it does not stop there. We reach out, expanding our circles, sharing with others. It does not matter if we never return to Pena Blanca Canyon. The experience travels well.

*Betty has been a full-time RVer since 1993. When her husband, Lin Strout, died of cancer in 1999, she chose to remain a nomad, a lifestyle that suits her. But the most important reason for staying on the road was the community of friends she found there. Betty also contributed "Going It Single."*

*New to full-time RVing, Donia explores the total freedom,
the endless variety, and nonstop learning of
living on the road.*

# Why We Like Full-Timing

Donia Steele

IT'S A CHILLY OCTOBER NIGHT AT A KENTUCKY STATE PARK *in the Appalachians. A young park ranger sets up her tape deck in an open-air pavilion. Mark and I sit on bleachers—another retired couple on one side of us, a homeless tent-camping family on the other. Three of the homeless children now dance exuberantly to their own beat on the wooden dance floor. My foot starts tapping to the music. A 5-foot-3 truck driver named Shorty and an earnest third-grader both want me for a partner, so I have a delicate decision to make. Five months ago I was dressed in a business suit, sitting in meetings to decide the agenda items for visiting consultants. Now I am dancing the Virginia Reel with an eight-year-old Appalachian boy under a cold, starry sky. Pinch me, I must be dreaming. Oh, wait a minute—this IS our real life!*

## Total Freedom

The question is, how could we *not* like this fantasy life we are leading? To be "off the clock" for the first time since college is like being reborn with a whole new identity. It's a recreational witness-protection program, minus the evil hit men. As retired full-timers, we are liberated not only from the meetings, memos, and office politics of the workplace, but also from yard work, house chores, traffic jams, and the millstone of too much furniture and other possessions.

Of course, the flip side is, we have also left behind our comfort zone, the easy world of knowing where everything is and what's going to happen when. On the road, it's Anything Goes: You get lost, things break, places don't turn out the way you thought they would be. You're always having to scrap your plans and do something else.

Coping with these conditions tests your flexibility and resourcefulness. You didn't realize you could change that tire until you had to. You get used to doing without things you took for granted before. You learn to loosen up and go with the flow.

## Endless Variety

Most people like having a place to call home, being a part of a fixed community. This is the feeling of "roots" that so many non-full-timers say is more important to them than the fun of roaming the land.

Mark and I feel just the opposite. We're happy as birds, trading an anchored lifestyle for the adventure of nonstop travel. We never tire of the changing scenery, following maps through unfamiliar terrain. The concept of "home" is an abstraction to us, at least for now. Each of us was born in one place and lived and worked in several others. None of these places did we ever think of as home. We have adopted the Escapees' slogan, "Home Is Where You Park It."

I always wanted to retire to a place of natural beauty, but I never dreamed of such variety. We camp beside a North Carolina lake glimpsed through tall pines. We listen from our Myrtle Beach campsite to the roaring Atlantic surf just over the dunes. In a South Dakota campground, our trailer window frames a stunning view of the jagged terrain known as the Badlands. Even the Badlands look good to us.

Out here in America's wide-open spaces, we revel in the big-dome skies that are a stage for weather pageants of every description. Talk about variety! Sun, shade, heat, humidity, wind, cold, clouds, rain—all carry more interest and impact than they used to in our climate-controlled world back home. You have never seen greens, purples, blacks, and browns like a Midwestern sky on a tornado day.

## Nonstop Learning

During our working days, the emphasis was not so much on learning new things, as on getting more efficient at the old ones. Now, no matter where we go, we always discover something we never knew before—about cactus plants, or RV weight ratings, or geology, or regional barbecue customs. Mark and I read all the brochures, study the exhibits, and say *Wow!* We take notes, even though there will never be a quiz.

Sometimes our exploring takes a deeply personal turn. We look up relatives we have not seen in years and some we've never met before. A distant cousin directed Mark to an historic storefront in Helena, Montana, where a plaque described how part of his family had been merchants on the frontier. One of my distant cousins showed us an area of rural Texas filled with places I had heard about but never thought I would actually see: my grandmother's girlhood home; a crumbling one-room schoolhouse where the family camped on deer-hunting trips; a cemetery tucked away in a stranger's back pasture, filled with the faded tombstones of my pioneer ancestors. We saw the grave of a girl who would have been my great-aunt, had she not died at the age of two.

We also learn fascinating things from strangers we meet along the way. We talk with truck drivers and waitresses, rock-shop owners and welders, ranchers and rodeo guys, and others so different in outlook and culture from those we lived among in suburbia. On one memorable evening in Copper Harbor, Michigan, we shared a campfire and roasted marshmallows with a young neighboring couple. James drove a truck, and Laurie was a pharmacy technician. With our faithful dogs curled up at our sides, we reminisced far into the night about the past dogs in our lives that we had loved and, finally, lost.

I thought about all the nights, going back maybe 20,000 years, that small nomadic groups must have spent huddled around fires with their domesticated wolves, gazing up at the same stars overhead. Could it be, we RV full-timers just inherited an extra measure of the wandering spirit from our early *homo sapiens* ancestors?

*Excerpted from* Steeles on Wheels, *an account of Mark and Donia Steele's early full-timing adventures, published March 2002 by Capital Books, Sterling, Virginia. After careers in journalism, book editing, home repair contracting, and house inspecting, the Steeles took early retirement in 1998. For more about their book, check out http://www.steelesonwheels.com. Donia also contributed "Eating Our Way Across the U.S.A."*

*Born and bred in New York City, Cathi compares living in the
great metropolis to living on the road. Then she never
left home without her Day-Timer; now she never
leaves the RV without her binoculars.*

# City Girl
# Takes a Hike

--------------------------------------------

Cathi Tessier

IN 1997 WHEN MY HUSBAND BOB AND I FIRST STARTED
preparing for an early retirement, we set our time line at three years and
began exploring our options.

The next summer, when Bob's young sons from back east came for
a visit, we rented a 28-foot RV and traveled with them up the coast of
California. Much to our surprise, the trip in the motorhome proved to be
a wonderful adventure. We loved this new way of travel and the conve-
nience of having our "home" with us. We felt safe and cozy and the ten-
day trip aroused new, unexplained feelings in us.

Upon our return home, we found ourselves drawn to RV dealers
where our questions might be answered. In a very short time, we considered becoming full-time RV travelers.

Having spent most of my adulthood living and working in New
York City, I knew life was about to change radically. I loved the hustle
and bustle of living in a large metropolis. The everyday things in my life
that comprised my comfort zone ranged from crowded commuter lines
to tall concrete or marble structures reaching to the sky.

Nevertheless, we went in head first, quitting our jobs, selling the house and all our belongings, taking off for places unknown. The contrast between my previous activities and those of a full-time RVer seems astonishing.

## ALL IN A DAY'S WORK

*Then:* *Waking up to the incessant ringing of the alarm at 4:45 a.m.*
Now:  Waking up to sunshine and birdsong whenever my eyes open.

*Then:* *Scratching my head wondering how I'll finish my report before the board meeting.*
Now:  Scratching my ankles wondering how those no-see-ums got inside my socks.

*Then:* *Collecting past due accounts.*
Now:  Collecting rock samples.

*Then:* *Learning how to use the new software installed on my computer.*
Now:  Learning how to hook up the new hitch we just installed on the car.

*Then:* *Knowing the location of the nearest fire exit in my office building.*
Now:  Knowing how to stack wood, teepee-style, for a roaring campfire.

*Then:* *Memorizing the names of my top ten customers.*
Now:  Learning the names of the different wild birds that visit my campsite.

*Then:* *Being a card-carrying member of the Credit Managers Association of America.*
Now:  Being a card-carrying certified Wildlife Observer.

*Then:* *Going to bed early on Sunday night to be ready for the workweek ahead.*
Now:  Not knowing what day it is.

*Then:* *Meeting the girls for lunch.*
Now:  Going down to the lake to feed the ducks.

*Then:* *Never leaving home without my Day-Timer.*

Now: Never going out without my binoculars.


*Then:* *Reviewing the monthly sales figures and estimating the month-end bonus.*

Now: Reviewing the map and estimating miles to our next destination.


## GETTING PERSONAL

*Then:* *Working out in the gym three times a week.*

Now: Taking a hike every day.


*Then:* *Noticing a run in my pantyhose.*

Now: Pulling burrs out of my socks.


*Then:* *Deciding whether to get a medium-curl perm or a relaxed wave.*

Now: Deciding which hatband to get for my new cowboy hat.


*Then:* *Being able to identify the subtle, passing fragrances of One, Escape, or Perspectives.*

Now: Picking up the scent of a passing skunk, a nearby horse stable, or a cattle farm.


*Then:* *Spraying weed killer around my lawn.*

Now: Sprinkling birdseed around my campsite.


*Then:* *Spending the entire weekend cleaning house and catching up on errands.*

Now: Spending a brief moment noticing how much dust accumulates when camping in the desert.


As I look over the list now, two years later, I can hardly relate to those events of my previous lifestyle as a career woman. When people grow up and live in one of the most sophisticated cities in the world, they tend to believe that they rank higher than their rural counterparts. They dominate fashion trends, Epicurean delights, and fitness strategies across the country. They hold themselves in the highest esteem.

My awakening came about like a bolt of lightening as I looked around me at the diverse group of women at various camping events. I encountered women from all walks of life, open and friendly, eager to make my acquaintance. While perhaps their field of expertise ranged from when to plant corn, make sauerkraut, bead a bracelet, or how to homeschool your kids, at the heart of it all, I found these women to be just like me.

I feel fortunate that my husband and I jumped into this adventuresome lifestyle. Our original plan was to work for part of the year and play for the other part until our pensions caught up with us. However, this lifestyle enables us to change course at a moment's notice and never miss a heartbeat. While we both previously enjoyed professional careers in the business world, we are delighted to take assignments in local or state parks where we can get to know the local wildlife. Or we can choose to spend a few months working amid the local community where we have met countless interesting people who are eager to learn about our "unusual" lifestyle.

People often ask if I miss having roots, if I long to tend my garden, if I yearn for the challenge of a career in a fast-paced environment, or if I wish I could return to "house" living again. Without hesitation, I can say that my roots are always with me; they reside deep in my heart. My garden is an ever-changing landscape of the current local community. When I look to each new day with eagerness and anticipation of the adventures I am sure to encounter, my biggest challenge is a fleeting concern wondering whether the day will be long enough to capture a rainbow. When nighttime arrives, I do not fall into bed exhausted from the fast-paced environment, but my heart and soul are filled with the warmth of the day's activities. And as I slip under the covers at night, I smile, knowing that I have lived the day to the fullest and am eager for tomorrow's dreams.

Would I give up the anticipation of a sunrise in Colorado today and a sunset in New Mexico tomorrow? Would I trade in the view from my window where I can watch a magpie train its young to fly in April and a cardinal splash about in the birdbath in January? Could I ever forget the joy of rescuing a goose from the entanglement of a fishing line or the surreal thrill of walking beside a coyote on a trail? Could I find anything more exciting than pulling into a campground where new surroundings will provide the unique opportunity to learn more about myself by learning more about others?

Could I trade the freedom, the adventures, or the exuberance of the unknown that lies before us, just down the road?

Oh no, not for a minute!


*Cathi Tessier was raised in New York City, a typical "Queens" girl: lots of makeup, jewelry, self-importance, and definitely big hair. She did little traveling and was happy to stay put. She and her husband both had health issues at an early age, leading to the decision to retire early and go on the road. She says it was absolutely the best thing they ever did for themselves. Cathi also contributed "Heart Place."*

# Side Roads

### FULL-TIMING THEN AND NOW BY JANICE LASKO

When we first started full-time RVing there were trials along the way. It was difficult receiving mail, staying connected to fixed-dwelling family and friends, getting cash (we had to visit banks before 3 p.m.), and medical support.

Today, communication with family and friends is made simple with cell phones and e-mail. Receiving mail can't be beat with the excellent mail services available. ATMs are everywhere. Money doesn't grow on trees, it comes out of walls! Medical support is still a challenge, but we carry all our records and x-rays (both dental and physical) with us. A side benefit of RVing, however, is you stay healthier longer.

### HOUSEWORK BY JEAN NELSON

I was getting tired of dusting things in my house, getting tired of cleaning only to do it over again the next day. I can straighten the rig in an hour or less. If it doesn't get done, it's no big deal.

### WHERE ARE YOU FROM? BY DARLENE MILLER

Where are you from? is a question we often get asked. We live full-time in our RV so that is hard to answer. I have lived in Iowa longer than anywhere but I have also lived in Michigan, Texas, and North Carolina. Our address is Texas but that is only because we need a place to collect our bills and occasional cards and letters. When we need our mail, we telephone the Texas RV club and have them send it by Priority Mail to General Delivery in care of the post office in the town where we are camped.

*After deciding to RV full-time, Terry wondered how she*
*could give up the treasures and keepsakes*
*collected over the years.*

# Grandma's Lace Tablecloth

Terry King

I'M A SENTIMENTALIST AT HEART. I LOVE NOSTALGIA, MEMENTOS, and keepsakes from the past. Though not a "collector" of things, I had amassed quite a few closet and cupboard fillers, heirlooms to me, that I just knew I could never part with. Some of the things I actually used on occasion like my grandmother's lace tablecloth, embroidered flour-sack dishtowels, and bone china cups. At Christmas time I brought out my Mother's jewel-eyed Santa mugs and her uniquely colored and shaped candy dishes. The old, big serving pieces were reserved for the holidays. Some other things I would revisit now and then and have my "remember when" moments: high school yearbooks, scrapbooks, and my children's baby books; the box of holiday cards, special school projects, and little handmade gifts from my children; significant books and memorable records. And I loved all of it, especially the way it made me feel inside, warm and toasty as if curled up with a favorite blanket and a steamy cup of hot chocolate.

When my husband Ken and I started talking seriously about RVing, I had no conception of what that would REALLY mean. I figured we'd make a few trips here and there and, of course, return to our little nest.

Little did I know he and I were on opposite sides of the traveling spectrum. But then, as we began traveling more and more in the fifth wheel trailer we had purchased, I too became consumed with the next trip route, the sights we'd see along the way, the Wal-Marts for stocking up and pass-through sleepovers, and finally the ultimate destination. The travel bug had definitely bitten me as well as Ken.

Then due to reorganization moves, I suddenly lost my job of eighteen years and wondered what I was supposed to do next. With Ken already retired, nothing was holding us back from taking longer trips more frequently. Our children were all married and settled. Though we had regular contact, they didn't need us now as they once had.

We began making bigger plans; our agenda included seeing as many states as possible and visiting all the national parks. I became less attached to my home and its contents and looked forward more and more to our next adventure. As we continued traveling, it became clear our home was a "bottleneck" for us. Even though we were not there much of the time, we still had the upkeep and maintenance responsibilities. So we decided to sell it.

And then I really panicked. How do I give up these roots? We had lived in our home for thirty years, the only home we'd ever had. We had raised our three children there, loved our neighborhood, our friends, our church, and all that surrounded our lives in this community. At first I couldn't conceive of selling it. However, practicality won out over emotional sentimentality and thirty days later we were "homeless." Thank goodness it sold that quickly or I might have changed my mind.

And then the task began. What do I need to keep for this new lifestyle, what do I need to keep for our children and grandchildren, and what MUST I part with forever? That was the scary thing, the "getting rid of" part. What was important to me, really important? Before I made any decision about the things in my home, I took some time out and thought about the trips we had made the past few years. My mind drifted to watching gorgeous sunsets reflecting soft pastel pinks, lavenders and oranges splashed with fiery reds and purples; climbing spiraling staircases to the tops of lighthouses for incredible ocean views; driving through drippy, dark and moody rain forests; going around curvy mountainous, heart-stopping roads that gave way to spectacular scenery; driving through areas of unusual and seldom seen wildlife; and getting immersed in new lifestyles and cultures in various cities.

But what touched my heart the most were the people experiences. We met such wonderful, friendly and caring people on the road, willing to help, no matter what the situation. When we were stranded on I-10 with a flat tire on our rig, it was another RVer who stopped to help. Some of the other experiences I remembered: coming to an RV park and our neighbor inviting us in for coffee; sharing books and conversation with others while doing laundry; listening to a stranger tell us about the loss of a family member and comforting that person with a hug; and worshiping in a small town church where every member welcomes us with a handshake, a smile, and an invitation to return.

It became very clear what was really important to me. We packed up our house quickly, gave many things away, had a huge garage sale, and gave all our furniture to our children who had just bought homes. And those mementos and keepsakes that were so important to me? Well— they still are. The things I absolutely could not part with are now safely packed away in boxes at my daughter's house awaiting my return. And when we finally hang up the keys, my grandma's lace tablecloth is coming out and you can bet I'll be browsing through those picture albums, baby books, and that box of mementos from our children's school days, while sipping hot chocolate in one of my bone china cups.

*Terry King says that being fifty-eight does have advantages: a wonderful marriage of thirty-six years, three beautiful married daughters, and six fantastic grandchildren. A degree in criminology gave her great jobs: social worker, drug half-way house counselor, and finally human resources director the last eighteen years. Now Terry and husband Ken live in their fifth wheel and travel.*

*After planning to go on the road for two years, Cindy and
her husband were unprepared for what
happened on the first day.*

# First Day

Cindy Cook

OUR FIRST EXPERIENCE IN AN RV WAS BARTERED. A USED parachute (for aerobatic pilots) was exchanged for the use of a friend's motorhome over the weekend. We never did get the fridge to work and about froze to death (in Florida?) at night. We slept in our clothes and made pillows out of towels, because we didn't know we were supposed to bring our own bedding.

"Isn't RVing great?" we said to each other as we agreed to make this our new lifestyle. Sure, give up two perfectly good jobs for a nomad life on wheels. We were about fifteen years younger than everyone we knew in South Florida. They all smiled, gray-haired and wrinkled from so much sun. No one thought we were crazy. "Go while you still can," they said.

It took two years to unload all our "stuff": real estate, furniture, mementos, airplane parts. Yes, airplane parts. No way could we carry those with us.

We lived in our RV for one month before the big "trip," to see if we could tolerate each other in such small quarters. By the end of the trial period, we couldn't wait to get rolling.

Finally the big day we had dreamed of arrived. Five minutes after we hit the road, a garbage truck pulled out in front of us. We stopped in time to avoid crashing. Our hearts were pounding, but still pumped with adrenaline.

For lunch, we pulled over into a rest area and walked back to our trailer. "Can you believe this? Everything is right here!" How clever.

We decided to camp at an ultralight airpark we'd been meaning to visit. In the process of parking, our trailer met with some rubber roof-eating tree branches. (We didn't suspect damage until one rainy day, but that's another story.) We had no hook-ups. It got real cold. We ran the furnace, the fridge, a bunch of lights and soon everything became quiet and dark. Our batteries had died. My mother had given us a silly little battery-operated lantern to use for "camping." We used it the rest of the night. We were happy and free and that's all that mattered.

Seven years later, we are still happy and free. But now we have solar power so we no longer run out of electricity.

*Cindy Cook has been full-timing happily for seven years now with her husband Jim. She has made many fine friends on the road and is finally using more creative sides of her talent, thanks to the full-timing lifestyle. Cindy also contributed "Cape Breton Isle" and "Special Places."*

# Side Roads

## DO I REALLY NEED IT? BY JEAN NELSON

When the urge to splurge hits, I have to ask if I really need this thing. What can I do to feel useful to myself and others? What creative things can I do that can consume my energy and time? What is my passion?

## DOWNSIZING BY LUCILLE TILLOTSON

Seven years ago our financial advisor planted the seed of an idea in our heads—we could retire in ten years and live off our investments. The dream of traveling full-time was born and is now becoming more of a reality. I bought my husband a retirement countdown clock for one of his significant birthdays to help keep us focused on that long-term goal. We've been reading, studying, and corresponding to learn all about this lifestyle. As we prepare for full-time RVing, we'll have to choose what to keep, get rid of, or store.

Not only do we have to downsize our personal stuff, we will have to eventually downsize our pets. We have had St. Bernards for years. They truly are sweet and loveable, gentle giants, but large animals and small spaces equate to frazzled nerves. (One of our Saints even had her own tent—she had more room than we did!) Some breeds need space to roam and freedom to run. As much as we care for our critters and love having them around, it would be uncaring on our part to expect a large exuberant dog to adapt to a much-changed lifestyle. But as long as we have our current furry critters, they will continue to be a part of our family and will be spoiled rotten until illness takes them away. We may have to temporarily modify the itinerary to accommodate our "slobber-chops."

*For Kim and her husband, the pleasures
of traveling go beyond visiting
beautiful places.*

# Treasures of Traveling

## Kim Swords

ONE OF OUR EARLIEST TRIPS ON THE ROAD WAS A TWO-MONTH journey from Denver to the Pacific Northwest. From there we traveled up into Canada to see Banff and Jasper. Our return trip took us through Glacier National Park and the Tetons of Wyoming.

You can imagine all the gorgeous scenery we encountered: glacier-covered mountains; lakes of emerald green; dense rain forests of old-growth trees dripping with ferns, lichen, and moss; fog-drenched beaches; and tidal pools filled with starfish, colored purple and bright orange. We encountered moose, black bears, herds of elk, mountain goats, three-foot-long salmon, and a profusion of wildflowers. We brought back rolls of film with incredible photographs of the majestic lands we visited.

Yet, to everyone's surprise, what we talked about most was the wonderful people we met on the road. At every turn strangers opened their homes to us, welcomed us into their gatherings, shared their time and resources with us, took time to offer assistance, and became our friends.

One particular day we were camped in Olympic National Park. We had a magnificent view, perched on a cliff overlooking the Pacific Ocean. Out on a stroll, my husband noticed men cleaning small silver fish at the fish-cleaning station in the park. Curious about what these small fish were called, my husband struck up a conversation with the fisherman. They were delighted to teach him all about smelt, including how to catch, clean, and cook them. Rick returned to our campsite with a bucketful of smelt the fisherman insisted we try. We were invited to stop by their campsite, which we did, eager to thank them for the smelt, which turned out to be very good and not fishy tasting at all. They introduced us to about twenty folks at the gathering and insisted we join them for the evening. The next day they insisted we join them to learn to catch smelt and for another evening of stories around the campfire.

For three days we were urged to join them in fishing, barbecues, and storytelling. So we did. All were relatives of the Williams family. They held an annual family reunion at this park once a year during the running of the smelt. At first we felt like outsiders and that we shouldn't be at a family reunion. But everyone insisted we stay and it was obvious they were delighted when we agreed to join them.

As we were leaving the area we exchanged addresses and promised to write. Rick and I agreed, "What a special family, so warm and friendly." We traveled through six states and two countries and everywhere we were amazed at how friendly, how generous, and how caring complete strangers were to us.

We left Colorado to see the natural wonders of the great Northwest and returned with our hearts filled with new friends and a profoundly deep knowledge of the goodness of human beings.


*Kim Swords and her husband Rick have traveled off and on in their motorhome for the past ten years.*

*According to Nicky, not all addictions are bad for you.
But, according to her husband, hers
could be bad for the RV.*

# An Addiction

Nicky Boston

I HAVE AN AWFUL ADDICTION BASED ON AN IRRATIONAL
fear. Some day, some time, some place, I'm going to run out of books to
read. I've carried this fear into our RVing lifestyle and have caused my
husband to insist that our rig not only lists to one side, but I'm solely
responsible for any overweight conditions on any of the axles.

It started innocently enough. I've always been an ardent library pa-
tron. Each week I made a stop at our local library, lovingly picking out
ten to twelve books that I would eagerly take home and devour. In my
thirties, I had a kind of reverence for the printed word, thinking that all
books I started had to be finished. In my forties, I gave myself permission
to give up on a book if I hadn't been truly enraptured by the fifth chapter.
In my fifties, that requirement diminished to the third chapter.

I preplanned each vacation with the help of the friendly library,
finding all sorts of out-of-the-way places en route, along with some fascinating side trips once we'd reached our destination. The travel books from
the library enabled our family to pick and choose our itinerary.

When we decided to adopt the RV lifestyle, I made a special farewell
visit to my local library. I gave each librarian a huge hug, threw a kiss to

my favorite bookshelves, and left with a warm glow full of remembrances of many an hour spent walking up and down the aisles looking for the perfect book for my mood.

I knew when we left that I would have to give up hardback books and pretty much stick to paperbacks. "Weight," my husband said sagely. "Weight," I agreed. So we left on our adventure with one book each.

At the first campground, I eagerly approached the exchange bookshelves. "Trade one for one of like kind," the sign declared. And I could appreciate the signage as I was faced with eight shelves of Harlequin Romances. My heart started to race and I could feel the tension start in my body. But wait a minute; some of the Harlequin Romances were labeled "Historical." I grabbed two, explaining to the empty air that I'd be back tomorrow with something to exchange. I returned the two books several days later, sheepishly looking over my shoulder to see if anyone noticed what I was doing. As far as I was concerned, my worst fear had become reality.

At the next campground there were a couple of shelves devoted to murder mysteries and Cold War spy novels. Every day I took one and slowly filled a shelf in the RV. My moods demanded a choice, I told myself, while secretly dreading the book exchanges filled with Harlequin Romances–Historical. After several months I had filled the upper shelves on one side of the bedroom with books. Soon I had enough books to fill one side with fiction and the other side with nonfiction. But this is it, I told myself. Just enough to have some choices. Just enough to catch up on all the authors I'd meant to read over the years.

"When is it enough?" my husband inquired.

"Oh, you can never have too many books," I assured him.

"Well, it's not as if the campgrounds don't have books," he responded.

"I know," I said.

"And what about the weight? You have to give up some of these."

"Oh," I replied airily, "I've made sure the weight is distributed well," thinking of my fiction and nonfiction sides in the bedroom. He retreated grumbling.

One evening he said, "You know, I feel like reading a Tom Clancy novel. Do you have any?" I gave him a choice of four titles. He picked one, muttering under his breath as he settled down for a good read. And as I picked up my book, I just smiled.

*Nicky Boston, a retired, full-time RVer, is an avid beader, who also loves reading, hiking, sightseeing, and knitting. Nicky and husband Don are volunteer builders for Habitat for Humanity Care-A-Vanners and members of the Escapees RV Club's "Awesome Parking Crew." Four daughters and five grandchildren are scattered through California and Texas. Nicky also contributed "September 11" and "The Survey."*

*Editors' note:* Nicky is not alone. According to the dictionary, there are many others afflicted with the same fear. They're called abibliophobics.

*Travel paints a detailed picture of lands never before seen.*
*In addition, for Alice, connecting with local*
*communities deepens and enriches*
*the experience.*

# The People
# in Between

-----------------------------------

Alice Zyetz

AS WE WERE SHOPPING FOR THE LAST TIME IN THE *GIGANTE* supermarket in San Miguel before we left Mexico, a woman came up to us and said, "It was such a pleasure having you here. I wish you a safe journey back to the States."

She looked familiar, but I couldn't remember her name or where we had met. Was it through folk music, bridge, little theater, play-reading, Torah study, Unity meditation, Unitarian services, singing for the children at the *Biblioteca*, ushering at the jazz festival? As I ran through the checklist, I realized how much we had become part of the community in the three months we were there, even though we also found time to be tourists, attending Mexican fiestas, sightseeing, and socializing with the people in our RV park.

Besides the freedom of RVing, the beautiful scenery, the other travelers, and the sightseeing, I love the ability we have to meet local people and get a sense of their life. I grew up in New York City and moved to Los Angeles when I was twenty-five. I had met people from some of the states in between and read books about them, but I never really could picture their lives until I started traveling. I had to be in

Mountain View, Arkansas, to see the eighty-year-olds and their great-grandchildren dancing traditional square dance patterns to the music of the folks in their well-worn overalls, who were playing fiddles, banjos, guitars, and harmonicas. Or meet the fisherman on the wharf in Inverness, Nova Scotia, where we were parked, who gave us fresh mackerel because he had extra and wanted us to experience the taste. We couldn't miss sharing pizza in the dining room of the square dancer couple in Tehachapi, California, who invited us to stay on their property when we called asking if they knew of a large Wal-Mart parking area where we could stay the night.

We connect with the local communities through our main interests: bridge, music, square dancing, and Jewish congregations. We have national directories for all four and when we have access to the Net, we can find even more information—actually too much information. Other travelers I've met establish a local presence by pursuing their own interests: twelve-step communities, various churches, Habitat for Humanity builds, contra dancing, compassionate communication circles.

Bridge was always a friendly game for us. When we lived in our stick house, we had a group of sixteen regulars and met once a month in someone's home. We played seven rounds of bridge, ate seven rounds of snacks and desserts, and caught up with each other's lives in between mouthfuls. When we decided to go on the road, we knew we would miss the regular bridge playing so we practiced going to bridge clubs in Los Angeles to get our fix. We were devastated. First of all we were strangers. Nobody smiled. The only thing they talked about was what they should have done in the previous hand. We were there to hold the cards so they could beat us, which they did rather consistently. One time we won big on one hand (out of twenty-eight) and I had the audacity to look happy. Big mistake. The opponents argued with each other about who was to blame for this unfortunate circumstance. For a long time we avoided playing in clubs, but we were desperate. How delightful to discover that in other parts of the country, the bridge players welcome newcomers and thank us for coming.

One bridge highlight was in Mammoth Lakes, California. We had planned to spend a few days sightseeing. Looking through the local paper,

I discovered that there was a bridge group meeting the next night. We went and found a group of people who played several times a week, had potlucks, socialized together, had lessons once a week. The teacher even had a huge awning he set up and invited us to join the group to watch the local Fourth of July parade. We dragged ourselves away ten days later only because we had a big family gathering to attend. We were in people's homes, had a sense of their lives, and knew we would always be welcome to return.

Our music also serves as a gateway to local people. We both sing and play folk instruments. Over the years we have accumulated a diverse repertoire (about four songs per genre) so that we can fit in with most amateur musicians we find. In Tecopa, California, we played in a pick-up dance band with other musicians who were passing through. In Port Aransas, Texas, we saw a sign for a jam session at the local bar, joined them, and had a great night of music. I am not a beer drinker, but that night it seemed appropriate to keep my throat moistened with a bottle of Shiner Bock, Texas Hill Country's best.

We lead singalongs. We were at a campground in eastern Washington and the manager told me that he used to play guitar. When I offered him mine, he declined saying that he wouldn't remember anything. I insisted and of course he played better than I ever will. The next morning his wife came by to thank us for the music, not only for the singalong, but also for encouraging her husband. She went on to say that their daughter had been killed in an accident the year before and this was the first time since then he had made any music.

One Saturday in Minnesota, we had stopped at a living history exhibit and spoke to the singer-storyteller who had been performing. He plays music at his father-in-law's church and invited us to come and play old gospel music with them the next day. "Just park your RV on the church grounds tonight," he said. There we were the next morning, in a little country church, leading "I'll Fly Away" and "Amazing Grace" and this was years before *Oh Brother, Where Art Thou?*

One of the biggest challenges for me as a Jew was the lack of religious community. Although born Jewish, I didn't find community until I was forty when I joined a temple in Los Angeles and became involved in the choir and adult study, as well as with a *Havurah*, an extended temple family. I knew full-timing would leave a gap in my traveling life, since there are relatively few Jewish RVers.

I did have some disappointments. One year I failed to buy the special-sized Hanukkah candles when I was in a Jewish neighborhood a few weeks earlier. So there I was in a market in a small town the night before and the checker told me to ask the manager who sent me over to the section where they sold votive candles, since those were the only religious candles he knew. Okay, birthday candles did work although they wobbled a bit in the *menorah*, the special candelabra. I just had to make sure I didn't move the menorah, kept it away from the window blinds, and watched it very, very carefully.

Another year at Passover, I wanted to be at a family *Seder* in someone's home as I had been every year since 1966. We were in Florida at the time and didn't know anyone in that area. So I started calling temples, but all they had available were large catered dinners at hotels, which lacked the family spirit I was seeking. I was disappointed. I knew if it were my temple's office and a traveler was asking to be included, they would have called any number of families who would have gladly made room for the stranger. But it was not to be and I felt bereft. I finally called a Jewish bookstore and must have sounded so needy that the woman I spoke to took my name and said she would see what she could do. She called back and said that her in-laws couldn't come to the small temple Seder and would we come in their place. We were introduced to many people, made to feel very welcome, and asked about our life on the road as wandering Jews.

After those experiences, I realized I needed to be more proactive. I stocked up on Hanukkah candles, *gefulte fish*, and matzoh ball ingredients whenever I saw them, bought a book called *Traveling Jewish in the USA*, and subscribed to several Internet newsletters so I could study Torah (first five books of the Bible) every Saturday no matter where I was. I also took advantage of Friday night services in areas that had small temples. Since these were small congregations, I stood out as an unfamiliar face. People would come over to welcome me and ask if I had just moved there. When they found out that I traveled and it was *my* one-ton Dodge Dually parked in the lot, they were even more curious about how a nice Jewish "girl" could love this lifestyle. It sparked lots of wonderful conversation.

Perhaps the richest experience for me was when we went to San Miguel, Mexico. We traveled to the Yucatan at the end of January and were planning to be in San Miguel around Easter for the celebrations. That year Passover came in the same week. On the way to the Yucatan, we met an American couple who were living permanently in San Miguel. Not to make the same mistake that I did in Florida, I asked (rather timidly) if they knew of any Jewish people in San Miguel. "Are you kidding?" they said. "There are two Jewish communities, one traditional and one more liberal."

I couldn't believe it. They gave me the names of two people to contact. When we arrived that spring, I called immediately and became immersed in the community. I actually went to both Seders, but my heart was with the liberal community. We had Torah study on Saturday mornings, some Friday night dinners, and an introduction to many cultural activities individual members were involved in. Of course Chuck and I sang with them, and they invited us to come back that fall to lead the music for Rosh Hashanah and Yom Kippur. Which we did—and stayed for three months.

And so our travels go. We've gotten to see lands in between Los Angeles and New York as well as some of Canada and Mexico. These places have come alive as people have taken us into their lives and communities. Our hearts are filled with the color of the landscape and the lives of the people have given it a depth we never expected. Our lives have been enriched; we hope we have done the same for them.

*Alice Zyetz and husband Chuck have lived full-time on the road since 1994. Their interests are varied. They love to travel but don't move very fast. People have commented that they leave "at the crack of noon." In addition to being co-editor of this book, Alice, while traveling, published another book,* You Shoulda Listened to Your Mother: 36 Timeless Success Tips for Working Women *(available at Amazon.com). Alice also contributed "The Saturday Solution."*

# *Exit Ramp*

## WHAT I LIKE ABOUT LIVING ON THE ROAD IS . . .

- the freedom, wondering who will cross my path tomorrow, and where I will be. *BC*

- the variety of places I live. *DW*

- seeing new places and then going back and seeing them again and again and again. *SE*

- new discoveries around every corner, being surrounded by the beauty of nature, and the feeling of anticipation as we pull onto the open road. *MS*

- the opportunity to see little towns, hidden treasures, talk to folks, and really smell the roses! *NA*

- you never know what adventures or new friendships the day holds. *SB*

- the unknown encounter that may be just around the bend. *CT*

- the new scenery and ability to get up and go at any time and change what the back yard looks like. *LE*

- the people we meet and the friends we make. *JW*

- EVERYTHING! *DE*

- having options. *CC*

- the easy lifestyle, many friends, and seeing this beautiful country. *DS*

# Life on the Road

Living on the road is more than a vacation. It is a way of life. Our writers share some of the unique experiences they have had living on the road.

*Although most aging parents with health problems are safely in a retirement community, Verna's 83-year-old mother and new husband were full-time RVers. Verna and Wally found themselves rescuing her parents from more than one misadventure.*

# Caregiving RV Style

Verna Baker

MOM LOVED RVING, TRAVELING FAR WITH HER SOLO RV FRIENDS. Then at age seventy-five, she had a major stroke. She worked hard at recovery, learning to talk again and even walk, but she never regained use of her right arm, her main driving arm. She was forced to "hang up her keys." She figured her RVing days were over, and for quite a few years they were. But then along came Tom.

Mom and Tom were married when she was eighty-three. Mom had enough money to buy an old trailer and Tom had an old truck. Actually all four of them—Mom, Tom, the truck, and the trailer—were in poor physical condition, but they put the dog in the back and took off anyway. As Mom said, "Just rattle your keys and I'll follow you anywhere." And she did. As it turned out, so did we. It was the beginning of our seven-year odyssey of rescuing Mom and Tom.

Now Tom was an inventive and hard-core boondocker, traveling with ladder, generator, solar panels, ham radio antennas, blue tank, and just about anything else he could put into or tie onto the rig. Most of these and the rig itself were held together by baling wire and duct tape. Our rescue missions were often of the repair type.

Once we received a phone message: "This is Tom. The dog got into some cactus. I pulled most of it out with pliers. She'll probably be all right. Your mother seems to have had a stroke so we're headed to your sister's in Reno. But the truck motor blew up so we got hauled to a one-casino town north of Las Vegas. We're parked out back. I think we need help." CLICK! CLICK?

Another time we were caravanning with them to the CARE Center in Livingston, Texas. At a rest stop, just after leaving San Antonio, Texas, my husband noticed that the holding tank strap was dragging. Pure luck and possibly divine intervention had kept the holding tank from tearing loose and spewing the ugly stuff all over the streets of San Antonio during rush hour traffic. It took several hours of inventive repair with the usual baling wire, duct tape, cardboard, rope, battery-powered drill, borrowed screws, and much unseemly language before we were on the road again. As far as I know that is still what keeps that holding tank secure. Tom considered that a temporary fix was permanent as long as it held.

Tom enjoyed creative fixing and was not into spending good money for fancy stuff, often to our dismay. When the old pickup gave out, he bought a flatbed truck. While his broken leg was healing (nothing stopped Tom), he built a cover for the flatbed. This cover was a wooden structure, much like a small garage. He had rigged up a cumbersome ramp and could drive their Subaru station wagon right onto the truck with a lot of advice and prayers from fellow campers. Now the car hung out only a couple of feet, but by chaining down the front end and the tires, and using heavy-duty straps, it was fairly secure. "Close enough," Tom would say as he hooked the bungie cord to his blue tarp garage door cover. It made quite a sight billowing in the wind as the whole outfit went down the freeway.

One of Tom's favorite stories, and he had plenty, was about being in an actual RV park. We had finally convinced him that since he occasionally needed to be on oxygen, they needed permanent electricity. Their generator was a sometime thing. When it did run, it usually needed more of the creative tinkering and forceful language. So here Tom was in a "real" RV park. He had set up the trailer and was now ready to unload the car. This usually took about a half hour of sweating and banging, often gathering quite a crowd.

"You should have seen this guy," said Tom. "I had just pulled out the ramp. And here he comes running around the back of his brand new, shiny trailer. You should have seen his face, white as a ghost, and his eyes were bigger than saucers."

"Are you going to unload that right here?" the guy sorta stuttered.

"Sure, no problem," said Tom, climbing in the car acting a bit shaky just for effect. "Now if you will just guide me from back there. I don't want the wheels running off the ramp before I get down, and I sure don't want to get going too fast and run into anything."

"Right," yelped the guy.

"But let me tell you, he sure was no help. Kept his eyes closed the whole time," laughed Tom. "Well, I put that car down, sweet as you please, with nearly a foot to spare between my rear bumper and his new trailer."

We followed and fixed as needed. We worried and fussed. But they sallied forth unafraid into the unknown, with Mom in her wheelchair and Tom on oxygen with his pacemaker and defibrillator. They hardly ever used a map. Amazingly, they always got where they were going—or close enough—sometimes sooner, sometimes later. "We weren't lost," they'd laugh after we found them. "We were just exploring."

*Verna Baker and her husband Wally are full-time RVers with a homebase in Coarsegold, California. They have three married sons and five grandchildren. The entire family has become reconciled to and even appreciative of their nomadic lifestyle. Verna is a retired elementary school teacher, who enjoys the freedom of RV living.*

*Usually when RVers take their morning walk, they return to
their RV. Janice wanted to try something different:
the RV was supposed to come to her.*

# I'd Rather Walk

Janice Lasko

SOMETIMES WHEN WE ARE MOVING THE RV TO A NEW LOCATION, I will leave our camping spot early in the morning to walk a route my husband and I mapped out the evening before. The plan is for him to finish derigging, hook up the toad, and follow a copy of the route toward our new destination. I'll walk in a forward direction with new views until he drives by in the motorhome and towed car (toad) to wait for me at the nearest turnout until I catch up to him. What a great idea! This arrangement suits both of us perfectly. He is able to sleep late, and I don't have to walk back the same route, something I find boring.

One fateful Sunday I started my walk about 5 a.m., expecting hubby to come for me three hours later. Eight o'clock came and went. I sipped my water and nibbled a power bar. Nine o'clock and still no sign of the rig. My mind was trying to stay calm, but my heart was pumping way too much adrenaline.

By 10 o'clock awful thoughts were screaming through my head. Had he been in an accident? Was he unconscious and unable to explain he had a nutty wife walking alone on the highway? Had I taken the wrong road? Had he decided to leave me and drive our full-time home in the opposite direction?

When 11 o'clock came and went, I turned around and started walking back toward our camping site, so I could see him coming. A light drizzle was falling, but I didn't want to hitch a ride back to the camping area because he'd never see me sitting in someone else's vehicle going in the opposite direction in the rain. Traffic was light; I probably couldn't catch a ride anyway.

It was past lunchtime and I was trying not to cry, thinking I only had a few coins in my pocket and no credit cards. Besides, I hadn't seen one restaurant.

What a dumb idea this was!

I heard the horn of the motorhome toot, toot, tooting before I saw it. I got in the rig, and off we went until we made a U-turn and went back to our campsite where he had left our toad because it had a flat tire as well as a flat spare.

He said he was going to come for me in the motorhome first thing, but then thought he'd try his luck at finding a tire store to take care of the exchanges. Well, this was Sunday and, in this semi-remote area, there were no stores open. By the time all this happened, the hours had ticked away and he had made no progress.

On Monday he took care of the tires while I soaked my feet. We spent another night camping in this area. I woke up Tuesday morning at 5 o'clock and took off on foot until my husband came by for me.

Wanna hear about the time we got lost on our bicycles?


*Janice and Gabby Lasko began RVing in 1985. When they weren't touring the country from back roads, they worked in ski resort communities. Janice became editor of* Escapees *magazine in 1998 and they lived in their motorhome at Escapees national headquarters in Livingston, Texas, taking only occasional trips. RVing full-time is the life for the Laskos, and they have just started to turn the wheels again, while Janice edits the magazine from a new vista daily. Janice also contributed "I Wish I Could," "Then and Now," "Favorite Place," and "People We Meet."*

*As she is holding up a line of fifty vehicles, Mary desperately tries to remember the height of her rig before entering a low bridge. If her husband were along, he'd know!*

# Stockbridge

------------------------------

## Mary Campbell

MY MEMORY HAS BEEN SLIPPING FOR THE LAST FEW YEARS; I hear that happens with age. But I will never forget Stockbridge.

The annual bicycle tour adventure in Michigan is called the Michigander. Each year my husband and I journey to the beginning of the ride, this year in Muskegon, and for a week we travel across the state, staying in various hamlets and enjoying the people and places. It all ends somewhere three hundred miles from the beginning.

While my husband is biking, I am SAGing, that is, supporting the thousand bikers. My rig holds one hundred gallons of water, which the promoters love. It is a great ride and the freedom I enjoy is fabulous, but one year that freedom came with a price—embarrassment.

I was traveling from one small hamlet to another when I came to Stockbridge. There are many ways to enter this little town in the middle of the state, but I chose the route that had a beautiful old bridge as the entrance to town, thus the name StockBRIDGE. As I approached the bridge and was about to enter, I noticed the small sign with white letters warning: 11 feet 10 inches. Picture this, my 39-foot Fleetwood Bounder sitting in the middle of the entrance to an 11-foot 10-inch bridge and nowhere to go but back. I racked my brain for information on just how high my rig was, but unfortunately that data was not forthcoming. I was in a quandary. Try for it and risk the wrath of hubby by ripping off the air conditioner on the roof? Or use my skills to back out of that situation?

By then there were about fifty cars in line trying to come under the bridge from the other direction, and about fifty cars behind me. Sooooooo, embarrassed as I was, I just started backing up ever so slowly. The wise folks behind me got the message and after the front traffic had cleared, the people behind me began passing me one by one as I backed up one by one. When I finally got to a cross street I could back into and turn around, I continued my journey to my SAG destination. Whew!

I'll never forget 12 feet 2 inches, the height of my rig. And 12 feet 5 inches is as low as I am willing to go for easy clearance. I'm glad I decided to swallow my pride and risk embarrassment. The rest of the journey was without incident. I hope that no local journalist was traveling my way at the bridge.

Except as an occasional conversation piece, I have been able to forget my adventure under the bridge. Maybe a faulty memory in later years is a good thing after all.


*Mary Campbell recently retired from General Motors in Detroit, Michigan. She and husband Tony are traveling the United States and Mexico in their 39-foot Bounder motorhome, volunteering for Habitat for Humanity, building affordable housing for those in need. They also volunteer for Disaster Recovery (tornadoes, etc.). At the time of this writing, they were leading a Habitat Build in the Mojave Desert where it was 103 degrees Fahrenheit.*

# Scenic Overlooks

## PISMO BEACH BY MARY SCHAAL

As I'm writing, aqua waves are rolling in and breaking into white foam on beautiful Pismo State Beach. It's in the low 70s with blue sky as far as I can see. A prehistoric-looking brown pelican is diving into the surf after its prey. My husband is enjoying a light on-shore wind by flying his stunt kite.

Pismo Beach attracts kite flyers, surfers, birdwatchers, beach-combers, chowder hounds, and monarch butterfly enthusiasts. The fall is the best time because winds and weather are mild, though winds can be upward of 20 m.p.h. at times. Monarch butterflies arrive in mid-November and stay through March. We've seen lots of birds as well, since it's along the western flyway. It's been fun to see hummingbirds and blue jays in November.

We walk the mile to town almost daily. Some of the best chowder made is served at the Splash Cafe. We order to go and sit near the pier, watching surfers as the sun sinks toward the horizon. All in all, it's Pismo perfect.

## OREGON BEACH BY SAMANTHA EPPES

One of my favorite places is a beach in Oregon. My dog, Gino, and I are sitting on a tall rock, near the water. The sky is gray, the water is gray, the air is chilly and smells of salt. Waves break over the bottom of our rock, but we are up at the top, well out of the water's reach. Except by the shoreline, the ocean seems quite peaceful.

There is a light fog, so the horizon is not visible. I put my arm around Gino as we stare at the ocean. Gray slowly surrounds us, but we can still see. His body feels warm against mine. We sit there, and, just for a moment, time stands still. We are safe. Nothing is wrong. Nothing can harm us. The only sound is the waves breaking on the rock. Gino leans his head against my shoulder. As the wind blows my hair, I know this will come to an end eventually. But for now, my soul is completely at peace.

*Remote Idaho seemed a million miles away from the events*
*of September 11 as Nicky and her friends tried to*
*make sense of the day's events.*

# September 11

------------------------------------

## Nicky Boston

IN A CAMPGROUND IN CATALDO, IDAHO, WE AWOKE TO A FAULTLESS
day of blue sky filled with early morning crispness. The Coeur d'Alene
river flowed by the front window sparkling in the sun. Our beautiful,
peaceful mountain was gearing itself for fall with a trace of color throughout the forest. Then we turned on the TV to catch the weather. And the
day changed.

In disbelief we wandered in and out of each other's coaches, neither
knocking for entry nor saying good-bye as we left. We eddied about the
RV park touching briefly as we passed each other, going back to the TV
to make sure the unthinkable had actually happened and yet hoping it
might have been a modern update of an H.G. Wells story.

About noon four of us took a bicycle ride on the trail alongside the
river as we needed a break from the ongoing horror. As we pedaled slowly
along, each in our own thoughts, a bald eagle disturbed by our approach
took wing across the trail in front of us and silently slid across the river.
The next bend revealed a red-tailed hawk gliding on an air current ever
higher. One end of a trailside pond was filled with a lady moose, reeds
hanging out of her mouth as she slowly chewed. She didn't seem afraid of
us, just kept her eye carefully on the strange two-wheeled creatures.

Going back to camp, we surprised a grouse on the trail. God's creatures seemed peaceful and undisturbed, and we had hope that life was normal. But nothing had changed. The news was still as horrific, the reality too frightening. We resumed our eddying around the park, going in and out of each other's rigs, grateful that we had each other as friends, companions of kindred spirit. We wished we could touch our family and old friends just to be assured that they were well.

We had no answers. We grieved under our faultless blue sky as the whole country did wherever they were. Maybe time will make sense of this.

*Nicky Boston also contributed "An Addiction" and "The Survey."*

*Living on the road since she was three months old, Samantha describes how she handles her stuff, friends, and schooling. She finds her parents "pretty cool— embarrassing at times, but cool nonetheless."*

# Traveling Teen

Samantha Eppes

I FIRST BEGAN TRAVELING WHEN I WAS THREE MONTHS OLD. Fourteen years later, I'm still traveling and still loving it.

We currently live in a Bounder motorhome, the better to hold all my "stuff." Stuff is a problem, but one of the few we face on the road. My parents and I are very close because we live in close quarters. Some see this as a difficulty, but it doesn't bother us; we're used to it. My theory is simply this: RVs aren't small, houses are big.

I am, of course, homeschooled. We're with a program called Calvert. I have to say, learning on the road has actually been an advantage. Though I don't particularly like school, I learn interesting things and receive a better education than I would in a group, as my personal strengths and weaknesses can be concentrated on. My parents often make field trips out of our travels. That way I learn additional things that aren't in my textbooks.

For instance, one of my school lessons asked that I write a detailed report about a subject of my choice, which had to be at least three pages long. The book suggested I consult an encyclopedia. We were starting a trip on the Oregon Trail, so I did a report on that. My report was twenty-three pages long, and instead of looking in an encyclopedia, I experienced the trail for myself. We did almost everything the pioneers did. I felt like a real pioneer, except my wagon had air-conditioning. We saw all the famous landmarks—Chimney Rock, Register Cliff, and my favorite, Independence Rock.

I liked Independence Rock because I got to climb it like the pioneers did. When I say climb, I mean it. There was no trail—just rock. That was a BIG thrill. The rock was shaped like a dome, but it was still very steep. That made things difficult and a little scary. Dad, the only brave one among us, had to help Mom and me up.

Things got easier once we reached the top, but not any less thrilling. There were plenty of ridges to use to climb up there, and there's nothing like jumping a crevice or two (no matter how small) to make your blood pressure skyrocket. I had a ball climbing around on the top, the wind in my hair. It was very windy, but what a spectacular view! As I slowly became more adventurous, I began to lead the way, and soon I found the highest point on the rock. It was very exciting to stand there, able to see for miles. I'll never forget it.

Coming down the rock was another story. I don't think my knees will ever be the same. But, on the bright side, my heart got more exercise than ever before as I looked at the long, steep descent I was about to make. We made it down safely with help from Dad, who once again was the only brave one. Then we went back to the rig where Mom and I promptly collapsed.

Yes, we are quite the adventurers. I don't do very well if I'm doing a lot of exercise for the first time in a while, but if it's routine, I'm fine. I love hiking, climbing rocks and trees, and running with my dog on the beach. In fact, most of my favorite places are in nature, with the exception of Las Vegas and Disney World.

I am almost never bored. Traveling is fun, and there's rarely a dull moment. When we're actually driving, we try to take a scenic route. That way we can admire nature. If it's not that pretty, we can play music, or chat, or read. Mom reads aloud to us because she doesn't get carsick easily. When we're staying in one place for a certain period of time, we can do whatever is fun in the area or socialize with friends.

A great many of our friends travel like us. We belong to an organization of full-time RVers called the Escapees, also known as SKPs.

I have many friends close to my age all over the country, with whom I keep in touch via letters or e-mail. Though I enjoy playing with other kids as much as anyone my age, I also can be equally comfortable and happy socializing with a group of adults. My parents' friends in the SKPs are my friends as well, and I can easily take part in an "adult" conversation. This is probably due to spending much of my younger years around the SKPs, who crammed good vocabulary and grown-up behavior into my head before my years. Thank you!

I am highly motivated to follow my dreams because of positive reinforcement from Mom and Dad. My family and I have a very close relationship. We're together almost all the time, so we're very honest with each other. I think it's fair to say they're my best friends. We go places together all the time, and, unlike most teenagers, I find my parents pretty cool. Embarrassing at times, but cool nonetheless.

We travel anywhere we please, making it easier to visit friends and relatives. I hate leaving old places, but the new places we visit are fun, too. Mom usually plans out our route and what we do when we get there. Dad always drives; Mom doesn't feel comfortable doing it yet. They look forward to the day when I can drive the RV while they relax in the back. Now they can't believe that day is only two years away!

We don't know what we'll do about high school and college, but that's still a ways off. In the meantime, we will keep traveling, living life to the fullest, and having fun. What could be better than that? Well, I must go; adventure calls! I hope to see you on the road.

*Samantha Eppes has been full-timing for fourteen years. She started when she was three months old and continues to enjoy it today. She currently lives in a Bounder motorhome with her parents and her miniature poodle, Gino. She loves writing, drawing, painting, and animals. She loves traveling as well. Samantha also contributed "Oregon Beach."*

*They thought they had learned from their previous experience of*
*being stuck in the sand, but Judy describes how it took*
*four of them to get the fifth wheel and truck*
*unstuck, yet again.*

# Stuck Again

-------------------------------------
Judy Francis

ONCE AGAIN, OUR TRUCK AND FIFTH WHEEL WERE STUCK—WITH
sand almost up to the axles on the fifth wheel. We were out in the middle
of nowhere, in the late afternoon, miles from a phone, with no cell phone.

It wasn't as hopeless as it sounds because we were meeting some
friends. Their fifth wheel was parked not far from where we were stuck,
but their truck was gone. We knew they'd be back; we just didn't know
how soon.

So how did we get into this mess? Because there was lots of open
space, we wanted to be respectful of their privacy and ours.

Our friends had parked in a large flat, open area some distance from
the dirt road on which we had driven in. There were some desert trees a
short distance behind their fifth wheel, a scattering of the ever-present
creosote bushes, and lots of hard sand. Having been stuck in sand once
before, Bill and I walked around the area, doing our best to determine
how solid the sand was. To our feet it felt very firm.

Finally we chose the "perfect" spot. Decision made, Bill climbed
into the truck and headed in that direction. As usual, I was on foot giving
directions. All of a sudden we both realized the truck and the fifth wheel

were sinking. Bill thought he had enough momentum to turn the truck and enough power to get both the truck and the fifth wheel back onto solid ground. However, in the middle of the turn, the truck bogged down. Now the truck and the fifth wheel were at a 45-degree angle to each other. Not good!

We hauled out shovels and the pieces of wood we used for leveling. Everything we did dug the wheels deeper into the sand. Time to stop and wait for help.

Bill went into the fifth wheel, which, much to our surprise, was reasonably level and made a pot of coffee. We pulled out chairs and sat down to enjoy the sunset. Way off in the distance were mountains that turned a gorgeous dark pinkish-purple as the sun began to drop below the horizon.

The sun was almost down when we heard the sound of Patty and Lyle's truck. After a round of hellos and explanations, we all decided it was too late to do anything that evening, that we'd do better in the morning after a good night's sleep. Patty invited us to dinner and we spent the evening catching up on all the news since we'd seen them last.

The next morning we surveyed the situation. Lyle suggested we unhook because it would be easier for him to pull us out if the truck were straight. Bill and I both said, "No!" We knew our rig and we knew that if we unhooked, there was a good chance we wouldn't be able to hook up again.

The men attached a tow rope to both trucks while Patty and I pushed sand away from the wheels so we could put wood in front of them. Both men got into their trucks and Lyle started to move forward. The rear wheels of his truck began to sink into the sand. This was not good.

Then I remembered that Bill and I had some carpet strips that we used as doormats. I suggested we put them under the rear wheels of Lyle's truck so they would have some traction. That worked. He pulled our rig forward a little more than the length of the carpet strips. The wheels of our truck and fifth wheel were now up on boards. We knew we'd be okay. It would take time but we'd be okay.

Yard by yard we inched forward, repositioning the wood and the carpet strips after each move. Fairly soon the men got tired of the slow pace and decided to go for broke. Patty and I moved away. Lyle and Bill revved their engines and Lyle's truck took off with our rig following. Bill had very little control—the most he could do was make sure the wheels on the truck were straight. Patty's heart and mine missed a few beats as we watched the truck and fifth wheel careen across the sand. They made it to firm ground, flattening a few creosote bushes on the way, with Bill waving his arm out the window of the truck and yelling, "Yee hah!"

One moral of the story: Two 150-pound humans can walk across ground that won't bear the weight of a fully loaded 30-foot fifth wheel and a Dodge Dually. More important moral of the story: Where would we be without friends?

*No longer a full-time traveler on the open road, Judy Francis has settled for the present time in the Midwest, although she still feels connected to the Sonoran desert and the red rock country of Arizona and Utah. She occupies time spent not working with family, friends, mysteries, astrology, and tarot cards.*

# Side Roads

### THE SIMPLE LIFE BY JEAN NELSON
We've been living the simple life for two years and ask ourselves from time to time if we miss the house. The answer is NO!

### CHRISTMAS ON THE ROAD BY CAROL TEBO
When we took to the road we made an agreement with our children that we would only buy Christmas presents for our nine grandchildren. Acquiring gifts for them as we traveled was fun and a way to share something special from the places and experiences we were having. We picked up jewelry, books, posters, t-shirts, calendars, and other representative memorabilia. None of the things was advertised on television or likely to be on children's wish lists, but those old enough to comprehend understood the gifts from Grandma and Grandpa would always be personal and meaningful to our relationship with them.

Long before Christmas and time to mail them off, the gifts for the grandchildren had already been lovingly gathered. As I wrapped and packaged them, I reflected on the circumstances of each purchase. For two people who hate malls, this brought the joy back into Christmas.

### MY FAVORITE PLACE BY JANICE LASKO
*What is your favorite place?* I am asked. You should see the smiles on the faces of the locals when I answer, "Where I am right now."

### SNOWBIRDS BY DARLENE MILLER
When our windshield was covered with frost and ice, we knew that it was time for these snowbirds to head our RV south for the winter. We had stayed longer than we planned because the weather had been so good this fall and early winter. It seems the further we travel south, the more clothes we shed. First I take off my gloves, then my scarf, then my hat, and then change to a lighter coat.

# Tecopa Desert Rats

Louie Adell

WE USED TO BE DESERT RATS,
Our nearest neighbors half a mile away on one side,
A mile on the other.
The barest of references made,
And we are transported back to it.
But now we have a check for $3800,
And the rig is gone.

Gone is the year of desert rat sunsets,
Vistas of sky,
Cities wide,
All to ourselves and the breath of the wind.
Roaming,
The time clock our own.
Hot springs and Buddhists, nudists and gnomes.
With old ladies soaking away life's achy joints.
And the desert queen,
Las Vegas—all glittering hot pink megawatt lights
and
All you can eat.

All the mountains you could climb,
That was our year in the rig.
E-mails and phone calls caught on the fly.
Always something new,
Because after a few weeks
We were gone.
New territory,
Discovery birthed in the sweet air of plenty of time.
Time was not an iron fortress,
It was a slow river
Bounded by sunrises
And sunsets.
We meandered slowly south,
Then slightly west,
Then slowly north again.
One crazy year-long river.

And now our life is a one-bedroom apartment,
Framed by a busy noisy street
And the corridor that goes past other apartments
With similarly framed people we haven't even met.

*Louie Adell and her partner Randy have traveled extensively in the United States, Canada, and Mexico, first in a truck and camper and later in a fifth wheel. They now live in Albany, New York, where they take care of her dad, who had a major stroke, and her mom, who has Alzheimer's Disease. Louie advises, "Travel while you can."*

*Traveling deep in Mexico, Nancy learns that when you're sick, never go to a hotel where they charge by the hour.*

# Sick in Mexico

Nancy Vineski

THIS IS THE TRUE, UNEXPURGATED STORY OF HOW WE CAME TO THE *decision that when one of us is sick, we don't worry about saving money and just use the credit card. Parental guidance advised.*

## PART I

Before we officially became full-timers, we traveled in a little pickup truck and camped in Mexico. One time, we're going down a little winding road and there's a guy hitchhiking. We now have a rule that we don't pick up anybody unless we both agree. But my husband Tom didn't listen to me then. He picks up the backpacking German tourist, who gets into the little Datsun truck with us. It's 90-something degrees outside. I'm in the middle. This guy has probably not had a bath in a month. I mean he has body odor you can cut with a knife. We're driving down the road with this guy and we haven't had any lunch. We come to a little village and ask if there's a restaurant. No, there's not a restaurant but there is a lady who serves food in her house. We knock on her door and she says, "Yes, I can make you some tacos." She has one plate already fixed which she gives to me. Then she fries up more tacos for Tom and the German backpacker. We have a nice lunch and leave.

We're driving down the road again and the backpacker says, "Hey, you guys want some good hash? I've got some really good hash in my backpack here."

I'm sitting there and all I can think about is *Midnight Express*. I'm going to spend the rest of my life dying in a Mexican prison. He's opening up his backpack and I'm thinking "Get this guy out of the car, now!" At that moment, the police stop us, just as the backpacker is reaching into his bag to pull out the hash. But Tom is wonderful. He gets out and talks to the policeman in his wonderful idiomatic Spanish. The policeman, in HIS wonderful idiomatic Spanish, says he stopped us because we don't have a front license plate and you have to have one in Mexico. Tom explains to the policeman that where we come from you don't need a front license plate. The reality is the policeman is trying to shake us down for a bribe. Little does he know he could have everything if he had just looked inside the truck. But Tom does such a good job of telling the policeman he's really a poor teacher and we don't have any money that it ends up where the policeman gets out his wallet with all the money he made by shaking down tourists. He tells Tom, "If you don't have any money, I can give you some."

He lets us go and we drive the German backpacker to the next crossroads and I finally assert myself and say, "You know something, that was just way too close for comfort and I hope I don't offend you BUT you're going to get out here." Tom stops and the backpacker exits. That's the last we see of him.

## PART 2

We stop that night to camp and go to bed right after dark. Tom immediately goes to sleep, and all of a sudden I start feeling sick—really sick. That night I have the worst food poisoning I've ever had in my life. I am in and out of the tent all night. I'm upchucking and going at the other end. Sometimes I'm upchucking and going at the other end at the same time . . . in the bushes. There is no bathroom, it is pitch dark, and Tom is snoring through this whole thing. I am so dehydrated, so sick. I feel like my ribs are broken from all the dry heaves because there's nothing left.

Finally after hours of this, I start to cry. At that very minute Tom wakes up! He says, "There, there, I'm here. What's wrong?" In between sobs I hear myself say in my little sick kid's voice: "I can't stand it any more, I've been sick all night, I have to go to a hotel, I have to have a bathroom, I can't crawl in and out of this tent one more time to go in the bushes."

He says "Okay" and we drive into Patzcuaro. We pass by a couple of nice tourist motels, but Tom is too "thrifty" to go there. So he finds a little hotel by the market that just local people go to. I am still so sick that I'm carrying the little bucket I'm upchucking into every ten minutes. We go into the lobby and the man asks Tom how many hours (!) he wants the room for. Tom says "All night." The guy looks at him with new respect. But did Tom catch on? No. He thinks "Wow, this is really great—only two bucks for a room."

We start up the steps and the man says "Oh excuse me, señor, but I'll have to give you this bucket of water because our plumbing is broken, and you'll have to flush the toilet with it." By this point I don't care any more. We continue up the steps and walk into the room. The glass in the windows is broken. It's filthy. I walk into the bathroom. Not only is there no water, there's never been water in the bathroom. There are no water pipes connected to the toilet or the sink. When you pour your bucket of water into the toilet, you can hear it coming out of the pipe in the wall going down to the gutter into the street below. Not to mention that no-body has cleaned this toilet that has no seat for years. I mean it was en-crusted with filth to the point where you'd never in your life even imagine that a toilet could ever get like that. There was nowhere in the room you could touch. I close my eyes and upchuck a couple of times into the toilet. We pour the water from the bucket into the toilet and listen to it go down into the street and I say, "I can't touch the bed, I can't lay on the bed, I can't do anything."

Tom goes down to the truck and gets my sleeping bag. He spreads the sleeping bag out on the bed. I lay on the bed with my upchuck bucket. Every ten minutes I lean over my upchuck bucket, and every other ten minutes I go into this bathroom. I try to squat over the toilet without touching anything. Tom is kept busy going up and down the steps getting buckets of water to throw this stuff out into the street. Motorcycle and diesel fumes are pumping in the broken windows. I am the sickest I have ever been. And all night long the headboard of the bed is going creak, creak, creak. On the other side the ladies of the evening are entertaining their customers and having inventive orgasms. They're screaming "Ahh, ahh, ahh" and I'm lying here grunting "Argh, argh, argh."

The next morning I am like death warmed over, but I'm not upchucking any more. I drink some bottled water we had. Tom is feeling really bad. I get a little sleep, and he goes down to the market. He comes back with a big sheaf of gladiolas, an empty milk bottle the shopkeeper gave him to use as a vase, a Sterno stove, and—from wherever he got it—a can of Campbell's Chicken Noodle Soup. He feeds me the chicken noodle soup and abjectly apologizes and says:

"No matter what, whenever we're sick again, we'll get a clean hotel room."

And that, honest to God, is exactly how it happened!

*Nancy Vineski was destined for greatness when she was born on Christmas Day at 1:11 a.m. and was left-handed, but, alas, terminal laziness and a compulsive book reading habit derailed her. After twenty-five years, more than ten full-time RVing with husband Tom, they are still traveling and she is loving (nearly) every minute of it. Nancy also contributed "Costa Rica" and "Arguments by the Number."*

*Driving down a winding road one night, Carol learned to relax and negotiate each curve as she came to it. She found this lesson also applied to her life as a full-timer.*

# Twists and Turns in the Road

Carol Tebo

ONE DARK NIGHT, YEARS BEFORE MY HUSBAND LARRY AND I MADE the leap of faith to become full-time RVers, I had a revelation while driving on a winding, unlit road. Anxious and tense, I was straining to see which way the road was going to bend. Finally, I decided to focus my vision just in front of my vehicle and on the solid white line along the shoulder. To my immediate relief, I found I could see exactly what I needed in time to negotiate any twists and turns in the road. I realized in that moment that this was exactly how I am supposed to live life.

Like all full-timers, as we prepared to embark on our new life we were asked myriad questions. Many of them revolved around how long we would RV, what would happen if we got ill, where we would live when we decided to hang up our keys. Though we acknowledged they were real issues, we couldn't see that far down the road (nor did we want to), so we gave dismissive answers. *We'll RV for as long as it's good. We'll deal with illness when the time comes. We'll get an apartment when we stop traveling.*

As I learned that dark night, we cannot negotiate a turn until we are upon it, so we chose not to expend our energy trying to look ahead. Our focus was on living every moment of our RV experience to the fullest. Our goal was to follow the road wherever it led, with no preconceived notions or guarantees of what lay ahead. For three years we had an incredible ride. Each curve in the road took us in a new direction filled with surprises and life-affirming lessons.

For eight months, as we learned the ropes of our new lifestyle, we gradually came to grips with the full import of our freedom. We guzzled everything in our path, often pinching ourselves to be sure it was real. "We did it! We escaped!" we would often squeal with delight.

Then, almost as if by appointment, our journey took a turn in the direction of one of the primary reasons for our becoming RVers—service. While spending time visiting and volunteering at the international headquarters of Habitat for Humanity in Americus, Georgia, we were invited to participate in a blitz build (building a number of houses in one week) in St. John's, Newfoundland. That exhilarating experience was the opening chapter of an intense eighteen-month period of volunteer work.

Besides two more Habitat blitz builds, we spent two months in Birmingham, Alabama, in the spring of 1998 doing clean-up and recovery work after the devastating tornado there; distributed food, clothing and household goods after a tornado wiped out the little town of Spencer, South Dakota; and repaired range fences, giving help and hope to farmers and ranchers hard hit by the previous winter's blizzards. The following spring we returned to Birmingham to build homes for tornado survivors with Habitat.

Our heads and hearts brimming with images and thoughts, the next twist in the road took us on another unanticipated course—we both began writing. In addition to a number of articles, I felt compelled to chronicle our experiences in a book that highlighted the goodness and caring we had observed in so many people, as well as the strength of the human spirit under duress. *Vehicles of Hope: Serving Others on the Road to Satisfaction* gives voice to the stories of nearly forty people. It will be published by 1st Books Library in the spring of 2003. Larry turned his attention to penning the novel he had always secretly dreamed of writing, which will be published soon as well.

In the fall of 1999, on the way to a winter camp spot where I would continue writing, we returned to Americus to visit Koinonia Partners, the communal farm considered the birthplace of Habitat for Humanity. There, the idea of partnership housing was first conceived and implemented. Our intention was to stay a week or two to help renovate the buildings that had fallen into disrepair. But as we learned more about the history and conviction of the place that seeks to be a "demonstration plot for the kingdom of God," we felt an unfamiliar tug at our hearts to stay and help get it back on its feet.

Our one-week stay stretched to three months, and then Larry was offered a position to help guide the revitalization of Koinonia. We found ourselves at one of those crossroads I had not wanted to imagine. Yet, if we were to stay true to our desire to remain open and receptive to life as it came to us, we knew we had to entertain the notion. We were surprised by how easy it was to say "yes."

For a year, we lived on the grounds in our trailer while I continued writing and Larry directed his energy to his job. Though we were happy when Habitat RVers stopped by to help and a little wistful when they pulled away, we felt certain we were there for a purpose. We knew we could hitch up any time, if we really wanted to.

Life has a way of continually prodding us, I'm learning. We were in store for yet another surprise—the opportunity to purchase one of the inexpensive, original Koinonia homes situated on a piece of wooded property—with a perfect spot for our trailer. This was by far the most difficult decision for me, because it represented permanence. However, I firmly believe that things happen for a reason and, once again, it felt right. Several months after moving in, Larry experienced health challenges that grounded him for a year.

I have had a lot of time to reflect on the road that brought us to this place. We have learned much about trusting, letting go of attachments, taking and learning from each encounter and moving on to the next "appointment." Consequently, we have been richly blessed. As we downsize our trailer in anticipation of more limited travel, I know one thing for certain: freedom is a matter of the heart, not of domicile. In our hearts, we will always be full-timers!


*Carol and Larry Tebo's work with Habitat for Humanity and at natural disasters during four years of full-timing form the basis for Carol's book,* Vehicles of Hope: Serving Others on the Road to Satisfaction, *to be published Spring 2003. Carol's other writings include* Blueberries from Heaven: A Basketful of Wisdom, *articles in* Unity *magazine, and a feature in* Rocking Chair Rebels, *published by Escapees. See http://www.tebotales.com for their Web site. Carol also contributed "Christmas on the Road."*

### THE COCOON BY MARTIE MOLLENHAUER

We had never been campers before so we didn't even know if we would like the experience. Rather than jumping in with both feet, we decided to look for a real bargain that our old, trusty 1987 van could pull. We found it. For $2500 we were now the proud owners of a Hi-Lo, which would be ready for us by Christmas.

We had so much fun figuring out what to buy for the trip and still be minimalists. We also had a challenge of where to store our "stuff." The Hi-Lo has very little cabinet space because the top comes down and fits snugly over the bottom half when traveling. Plastic containers became our bureaus, and the rest of our clothes fit beneath the dinette seats. Sure, we would have to make up the beds every day, but we loved the challenge. We learned about every type of sleeping bag available and bought matching ones. Once we started traveling, we would pull out the beds and unroll the bags every night. In the morning was the reverse. We chose two pots with lids, a frying pan, and mugs for our morning tea. Everything else was plastic or paper.

We named the Hi-Lo "The Cocoon" after waking up one morning and laughing at both of us sleeping in our bags, snuggly warm in our cocoons. We hope that we will emerge from this adventure as the beautiful butterflies within.

### A SURPRISE BY STEPHANIE BERNHAGEN

When we first began the full-time RV lifestyle, I was surprised to realize that there are still chores. It isn't an endless vacation.

### WELL-TRAVELED DOGS BY JANET R. WILDER

Our two mini-poodles have visited more places than most American humans.

*When things went wrong, Vicki was able to deal*
*effectively with each problem.*

# Unhitched in Nebraska

Vicki Kahn

WE WERE OUTSIDE OMAHA, NEBRASKA, PLANNING TO DRIVE east to our home in Pennsylvania and had stopped overnight at Thornhaven Campground. We were tired and had been careless about unhitching the car. That morning our plan was to drive separately to a gas station near the Interstate and then hitch up. Bill drove the motorhome and I followed in our old 1984 Honda Civic.

I hadn't driven too far when, all of a sudden, the tow bar on the Honda slipped down under the car; the car rose up and then bounced down hard, gouging the road deeply. I called Bill on the CB to come back; we had a serious problem.

The tow bar had come loose because the pins had been put in carelessly. Bill took one look and said we couldn't stop for repairs or replacement as it would take days longer and he wanted to get home. He twisted a wire coat hanger around both tow bar and car, checked the radiator and tires, and declared us ready to roll. We gassed up as planned and decided we would drive separately until we got to the first rest stop.

CBs still on, he drove the motorhome ahead of me. Suddenly the Interstate turned to the right and the sign said "I-80 Chicago East." He made the turn. I was in the wrong lane and couldn't safely get over there. As I saw him disappear down the road, I had my first panic attack. Would I ever see him again? What was Plan A and what was Plan B?

Silence met my calls on the CB. Thoughts raced through my head; I didn't even have a toothbrush with me. As I drove down the road to the next exit, I made all kinds of contingency plans. After what seemed an eternity, I finally got on the correct road going east. An assessment of my resources tallied included a bottle of water, some money, a CB radio, a tank full of gas, and an air-conditioned car with a good radio. As I adjusted to this new state of temporary singledom, I approached the first rest stop. Would he be waiting for me? If not, I would call the State Police. But thank goodness he was there according to our original plan.

We made plans for driving separately the rest of the trip, not wanting to trust the damaged tow bar. We would stay within sight of each other. If I needed a potty stop or coffee break, I would communicate on the CB. We slept in the motorhome in rest areas along the Interstate and were home in three days. I was very tired but proud I had been able to rise to the situation.

*In their year-long travel sabbatical, Vicki Kahn, an artist, had to adapt her work with clay to a small space. Of necessity, she miniaturized the process, used a small kiln, and discovered a whole new direction for her work: porcelain bead jewelry. Vicki especially loves working with porcelain. She says nothing else is as luminescent, brilliant, and sensuous.*

*Some RVers travel with a theme, like following the Oregon Trail, biking Rails to Trails paths, or getting to each major league baseball stadium. One theme for Donia and her husband is exploring regional eating places.*

# Eating Our Way Across the U.S.A.

Donia Steele

FULL-TIMING IS TRULY A MOVEABLE FEAST FOR PEOPLE WHO love food as Mark and I do. Lots of people who stay put love good food, too—but even if your home is surrounded by every possible kind of restaurant, there is no way to duplicate the experience of moving from place to place, enjoying distinctive regional specialties like Pacific Ocean Dungeness crabs, Amish shoefly pie, and Cajun *boudin*, right where they are grown, caught, cured, stuffed, or spiced.

It was a grand stroke of destiny when a friend gave us a copy of Jane and Michael Stern's *Eat Your Way Across the U.S.A.* as a farewell present. This modest paperback, a revision and expansion of the authors' earlier classic, *Road Food,* quickly became our travel bible. Although the authors do mention a few of their favorite haute cuisine restaurants, their primary focus is on the same kind of downhome places Mark and I would choose — homey diners, crab shacks, hamburger joints, barbecue pits, funky lunch counters and cafeterias, and home-cooking meccas with cracked-vinyl booths where the same waitresses have served the same customers for forty years.

Thanks to the Sterns we had fried green tomatoes at the original Whistle Stop Café in Irondale, Alabama; Chinook Eggs (poached eggs on savory salmon patties) for brunch at the Classen Grill in Oklahoma City; and cabrito (goat) tortillas at El Norteno in Albuquerque, New Mexico. We once spent two entire days in Memphis, trying out one barbecue place after another. Another time we drove two states away (a 220-mile round trip) to have lunch at Lambert's famous roadhouse in Sikeston, Missouri—"Home of the Thrown Rolls." You raise your hand, and a waiter standing halfway across the dining room throws you a roll warm from the oven. Honestly, how could you resist a place like this, when you're camped just 100 miles away?

This is not to imply that Mark and I can't find restaurants by ourselves. In fact, we have our own list of favorites we'd like to tell the world about. Mark's time-tested method for restaurant selection in a strange town is the Full-Parking-Lot Rule: Always go to the restaurant that has the most vehicles in its parking lot, even if it's surrounded by places that look better on the outside. Trust the locals; they know where the good food is.

Thus did we discover gems like the wonderful Onate Basque supper club in Boise, a place of heavenly food and timeless ambience. And the Main Street Diner in Buffalo, Wyoming, a naugahyde-stool joint where we lunched on world-class burgers, home-cut fries, and made-from-scratch tomato soup. And the Bluebonnet Café, a no-nonsense eatery in Marble Falls, Texas, where there are always so many customers lined up for the chicken-fried steak and banana cream pie that the staff has taken to seating singles and doubles at large shared tables in the middle of the dining room.

Sometimes it's the ambience that attracts us, as in the case of the inimitable Ajax Café on the waterfront in tiny Port Hadlock, Washington. We had heard about this place where guests are offered a selection of zany accessories to wear as they dine. But until you try it, folks, you can't imagine the silly fun of eating dinner in a General Patton helmet and polka-dot clip-on tie (Mark) or a fluffy chicken hat with long yellow feet dangling down like pigtails (that would be *moi*). And of course, you're surrounded all the while by other guests laughing at each other in French Foreign Legion caps, Abe Lincoln stovepipes, '50s pillbox hats with veils, and sweeping lavender feather boas.

By now you're probably getting the idea that full-timing is tough on waistlines. No question about it! We always plan to get a grip as soon as we leave the delicious region we're in, but it never seems to work out. *We'll eat light when we get to Michigan.* Except for a few different kinds of Cornish pasties at that pasty shop. Where else are we ever gonna get Cornish pasties? *Well, it will be easy to diet when we get to Indiana. What does Indiana have, anyway?* Yikes, forgot about that heaven-in-every-bite raspberry cream pie at Das Dutchman Essenhaus. *Okay, then Kentucky. For sure, we'll cut down in Kentucky.* Wait a minute—Kentucky has barbecue!

RVers just love to eat, period. They love Sunday-afternoon ice cream socials. They love sitting around the picnic table eating hors d'oeuvres while they cook out on portable grills. They especially love campground potlucks, featuring yummy creations laden with sausage, sour cream, hamburger meat, pasta, cheddar cheese, and especially condensed mushroom soup. Don't be fooled by the potluck variation known as a "salad luncheon," either. The typical salad is a molded gelatin dish made with whipped cream, fruit, and nuts—and half of the total array is desserts.

Naturally, Mark and I are big fans of campground potlucks. During our first stay at a Winter Texan resort down near the border, we invested in one of those insulated carriers with handles, which Mark calls our "Rio Grande Valley briefcase." It's indispensable for keeping a 9x13-inch casserole dish warm en route to the rec hall. Also, like many other RVers, we bought ourselves some large partitioned plastic trays to take to potlucks, because—let's face it—no regular plate is big enough.

*Excerpted from* Steeles on Wheels, *an account of Mark and Donia Steele's early full-timing adventures, published March 2002 by Capital Books, Sterling, VA. For more about their book, check out http://www.steelesonwheels.com. Donia also contributed "Why We Like Full-Timing."*

*If you have ever driven alone on a dark night, you might
have, as Sabine did, felt uneasy chills up and
down your spine and had dark thoughts
playing with your mind.*

# Dark Highways

Sabine Hartmann

I'M DRIVING DOWN A DARK HIGHWAY, ALONE. BUT I COULD
be on the other side of the earth, for all I know. I could even be in outer
space, or on an alien planet, following this road—a concrete snake curl-
ing out into the darkness. What proof do I have that I am where I think
I am? None. Or almost none: a map. And what more is a map than a
sheet of paper, covered with random colors and improbable names? How
could I feel confident and secure, protected only by this drawing, while
driving through the alien night?

I think back to what I read once about an old Indian chief. He couldn't
believe that the White man would go as far as to pretend that those lines
and colors on a little piece of paper represented the world. How could
anybody in his right mind pretend to pack all the high mountains, the wide
plains, the beautiful rivers and lakes, and the entire diversity of animals,
flowers, trees and humans onto this small square of paper?

Considering again the deserted road, which loses itself ahead in the
dark, how could one possibly pack all the darkness of the night into a
map, and still believe that twenty miles ahead would be a rest area?

Less and less sure about the certainty I had only just an hour ago, I
begin watching the shadows on the roadside. A tree? Or an alien totem

pole? A bush? Or an alien animal, crouching there, ready to jump, watching me as I'm watching it? An open space: a field, or a desert, or a lake? Who knows? I don't even bother checking with the map anymore.

Nothing looks like expected. It's not normal that there aren't other cars around on either side of the freeway. I must have gotten off the track someplace, taken the wrong turn, the wrong lane, and driven straight out into space, without noticing.

What will I do now? Just follow this deserted road to the edge of the world? And who knows if there isn't a real edge, someplace? Humans have only been so far. What if, after the next hilltop, there will be nothing but dark, empty space, ready to swallow me?

*Keep driving! Don't stop! If I stop, anything could happen.*

Yes, the stars seem brighter, nearer. I wonder how they made that road right to the sky. Is this the so-called "Stairway to Heaven"? But where is heaven? Shouldn't there be a bright light instead of so much darkness? Maybe I'm on the road to hell.

*Keep driving! Don't stop!*

No one ever proved that there were aliens out there. But no one was ever able to prove the contrary, either. It's like the monster of the Loch Ness: it's there, and it's not there, depending on whom you speak to. No one is able to prove its existence or its nonexistence. And there we are only talking about a medium-size lake in Scotland, whereas aliens have a whole universe to hide in. We little humans could search forever, without the slightest chance of finding them, if they'd decided to hide.

There, I've seen something move. A bush or an alien? Because— back to aliens—it's not proven, either, that they want to hide. They might be right here, in that pitch-black night, and I wouldn't know it. As little as I know where I am, by the way.

*Keep driving! Don't stop!*

A creepy feeling starts on my back, running up and down the spine. Not a good sign. Did I glance in the back of my travel van when I came in the last time? Every woman knows she should do that at night. But of course, I've forgotten. Anybody—or anything—might have crept in, lurking now in the dark, eyeing the back of my neck, ready to jump on me at any moment. My rear mirror shows only blackness. I wish I knew what's going on behind my back. I wish I could stop and check.

*Keep driving! Don't stop! The darkness holds many dangers.*

I wonder what will happen when I run out of gas. I'll have to stop then, in the middle of the night, in the middle of nowhere, in the middle of outer space. I wonder how outer space smells, feels, tastes. I wonder if there is a sound, or if it's just plain silence. I wonder what one can hear in hell, or in heaven. But this is only the "road to," and I still don't know if it's going to be either one of them, or an alien planet. I'd prefer the planet. It would be less definite than heaven or hell. I could make plans to escape. Of course, the aliens would roll in the road, so I couldn't jump in the car and simply drive back to earth. And first of all, I'd need some gas. Are there gas stations on alien planets? I think that escape will need some careful planning. Maybe I could steal a space ship from the aliens because they certainly have space ships. Could I learn to drive an alien space ship? How complicated all this seems. What shall I do? Where will I end up?

*Keep driving! Don't stop!*

There: lights. This must be the door to heaven, or the door to hell, or the alien's space-terminal. What shall I do? I'll just slow down a bit, get a good look before I bump right into "them."

There it is. I can even recognize several small buildings. I'm too curious, I have to check, just a quick look, just one look.

But . . . hey!

It's the rest area . . . !


*Born and raised in Switzerland, Sabine Hartmann left Europe in 1997 for North America. Married in 1999, Sabine and husband James have been living full-time on the road since then. Formerly a published reporter and "hobby" writer in Switzerland, she keeps working on her English to accomplish her hope: becoming a full-time writer in the United States.*

*Many RVers volunteer their time on the road. One child,*
*a victim of poverty and neglect, gave Hope the*
*vision to help others better their lives.*

# Making a Difference

### Hope Sykes

WHEN I WAS A CHILD, THE MAIL CARRIER WAS ABOUT AS CLOSE
as I could get to a traveling experience in the Deep South. From his old
Ford came letters from distant relatives or parcels whose wrappings con-
tained news from other cities. Entertainment for us was almost always home-
made, change was gradual, and vacations were merely time off from school.
For many of my neighbors, time seemed to stand still. For me, though, the
stillness created inner growth and an unquenchable wanderlust.

I didn't just want to travel. I wanted to give something back. How much
I might be able to do became quickly apparent with my first volunteer expe-
rience which would touch my heart and eventually guide me to encourage
RVers to volunteer once I gained the freedom to travel as an adult.

The time? The 1970s when I was very much landlocked and waiting
with all of the rest of my class to finish high school. You see in Dixie,
every school year gave the inevitable revelation of those who would make
it to the next school year and those who wouldn't. Some signs were obvious like the kids from the rural routes who arrived each day with no shoes
to the less obvious signs of child abuse, which were only discovered by
accident and through childhood whisperings on the playground. The

police were seldom notified. Parents just "got mad," which usually mani-fested in an assortment of beatings.

In high school, I signed up to be a teacher's aide at a nearby elemen-tary school and asked to go beyond the usual duties and design and teach a creative writing class. My wish was granted.

Of all of my students, Carolyn would be the one who would move me the most. She was the stereotype of the child who missed a couple of grades and didn't pass with her class. Her unruly legs never quite fit under her desk and her hair separated into long, greasy strands which the sun seemed unable to bleach despite her skin's testimony to her endless hours in pursuit of Mississippi cotton. Beneath her bangs, though, rode blue-gray eyes whose gaze I could occasionally capture. I felt optimistic.

The writing class, as it turned out, was a once-a-week break for all of us from the endless drill-and-practice exercises common in this small com-munity whose only entertainments were the summer religious revivals where shakers and movers could beat back the heat, humidity, and flies with the free hand fans from the nearby funeral home.

On my first day, I walked to the green cinder-block classroom where I would teach. The room always smelled the same way: burnt erasers — that was it — that mixture you get from Southern heat, the humidity, the aftermath of an elementary recess, and tightly-packed bodies. Thirty faces dripped perspiration alphabetically row by row. There was no air condi-tioner, no fan. The sole water cooler often ran hot and low after a hit by one or two of the bigger boys in the class.

I wanted to know these students. What did they love to do in life? What captured their imagination? Mostly, how could any of them find any real happiness? I found Carolyn that first day where the teacher had left her and the rest of the class writing "I will not talk in class" 200 times. It was the second time that they endured the task that day.

When I first entered the room, they all paused as I observed the Scruggs boy penning the lines in record time. I smiled. "Creative," I thought. He used the four-pencil method to write the exercise while us-ing pencils wrapped tightly with rubber bands. The students and I took the class simple and slow, which seemed to work for us. I finally grasped the chalk and put a few sentences on the board as story starters. Carolyn would periodically interrupt my sentences by wanting to know if I "smoked or chewed," but I kept going.

More blank faces. Was it the heat? Wasn't I able to reach them at all? Getting the first papers back, I checked them again and again. How could it be that most of this sixth grade class could barely read? When I checked for Carolyn's paper, it wasn't there. She sneered just a bit as she left.

Sessions came and went and Carolyn finally figured out that I didn't chew or smoke although I could see her staring off more and more in the distance. The class punishments by her teacher still persisted although they seemed to be getting less since the teacher had announced a wedding date.

The coming days would be different. I couldn't stand the competition of the rows and stares any longer. I began to arrange the class desks in a circle. NOT ALLOWED! SIMPLY NOT ALLOWED! That was basically all that I heard from Carolyn's teacher, but I held my ground and had the students promise her that the desks would return to alphabetical, perspirational order at the end of the session. Progress. The kids finally began to loosen up a bit.

I read to them. I talked to them. I asked them questions. Finally, they wanted to write. On a lark, I wrote SUNSHINE ON A RIVER. It would be one of the five story starter lines for the day. This time Carolyn turned in a paper.

As I began to go over the papers, I quickly discarded grammar after a cursory glance. That would definitely take more work, but the expressions from the minds of the authors were able to finally come through. As I read along, I vowed never to give a grade below a "B." Comments would be in pencil or a blue pen—never red. Carolyn's paper was next and her text covered a full page.

The river turned out to be her favorite place, her private place. No beatings, I bet. No siblings. To her, there was nothing like a warm summer day for staring at clouds, watching the river, and taking a long draw from a cigar. Not exactly Mark Twain, but there was literary promise. Sadly, I knew that what she was writing was probably true. The joy was real, but her loneliness was evident. I gave her an "A" and returned the papers next session. To my surprise, Carolyn was quiet the whole hour.

Later, a small hand touched my back after the class had ended. There had gotten to be a regular line of Do-you-know-what-I-did's. Carolyn had waited until the end of the line. She wanted to help me after class and I finally got that long look into those blue-gray eyes. They were crystal clear as we linked arms and headed to the cool outdoors.

Since that year, I often wonder what happened to Carolyn. I still see her in my mind's eye and treasure that spark, that connection. My life is dedicated to volunteering, helping others and letting other RVers know the impact they can have. Remembering Carolyn, I began working with student writers again. This time it was a virtual experience, via the Internet. Students and teachers were enthusiastic and the writing was fresh and vital as they tackled social problems and sought solutions within their own community.

Through this experience I am renewed and am reminded of Carolyn once again. If just one child felt listened to, saw beyond their environment to a future of possibilities, then Carolyn, too, has had an impact.

*Hope Sykes is a freelance writer. An active volunteer, she works to inspire a spirit of volunteerism internationally and strives to promote a United States mobile volunteer movement by RV. Hope also contributed "No Regrets."*

# Side Roads

### SCARIEST MOMENT BY MARY SCHAAL

My scariest moment RVing was riding in the passenger seat in rush-hour traffic through Los Angeles from Ventura to Riverside, especially when the formerly left-hand exit was changed without notice to a right-hand one, six lanes over.

### COSTA RICA VIA MOTORHOME BY NANCY VINESKI

At our first Escapade, in a Boondocking seminar, we shared the information that we had lived in Central America and Mexico and had traveled to Nicaragua. A very elderly couple in front of us turned around and the woman said, "Oh, I'd really love to talk to you. My husband and I are talking about driving to Costa Rica in our motorhome, and I've been wanting to find someone who has done it. You see my husband is 87, but I'm only 83 so I drive the motorhome . . . ." While she was talking, I was casting about in my mind trying to find a courteous way to say, "DON'T DO IT! ARE YOU CRAZY?"

Just as I was opening my mouth, she said, "Usually we don't go any farther than southern Mexico, but last year we took the mountain road over Tuxtepec . . . ."

That road is very mountainous with many switchbacks and no guardrails. After hearing that I said, "Oh, don't give it a thought. The only problem is three or four hours for paperwork at each border. Have a wonderful time. Here's a neat trailer park in San Jose, Costa Rica. You'll probably want to visit these places . . . ."

### SCARIEST MOMENT BY SAMANTHA EPPES

My scariest moment RVing was when a really big tornado was close by and coming our way. Luckily it changed course.

*Many people are amazed to find RVers who have been full-timers*
*for ten years. Ann met a couple in their mid-80s who had*
*been traveling full-time for sixty years and*
*were still not ready to stop.*

# On the Road
# For 60 Years

------------------------------------

## Ann Howell

IN THE WINTER OF 1987 WE WERE IN FLORIDA IN A SMALL
campground in Key West. A sweet elderly couple in a small fifth wheel was
parked right next to us. She was a beautiful woman, slender, with a very
pretty face, and had a beautiful head of chalk-white hair that she wore
coiled up on her head. I could have painted her picture; she was so distinctive. He was sweet and skinny with gray hair, and very much a gentleman.
Their names were Blanche and Herbert. We invited them over for a drink
and they told us their history. They were both from New York and had
gotten married in 1927. They decided to hitchhike across the country to the
West Coast. Now how many people would do that in 1927?

The first incident happened in Pennsylvania. Walking in a little town,
they got arrested. She was wearing pants in public, which was easier for
travel, but illegal in those days. Something had happened in town and
they were the strangers. After a while it was taken care of and off they
went, but they were a little surprised by this turn of events.

They traveled across country for a few weeks, but finally came to
what Blanche referred to as "that little place in New Mexico. What was
the name of that little place, Herb?"

"Albuquerque," Herb said.

When they got to that "little place" in New Mexico, they met a tribe of Indians. Blanche and Herb started talking with the Indians. After a few minutes the Indians invited them into one of their buildings. When they went in, their hosts closed the doors and locked them in. The tribe couldn't speak English, and although Herb and Blanche thought they had been communicating, they weren't sure how well they had succeeded. But now they were a little bit scared because they had no idea why they had been locked inside the building for almost two hours. They noticed a lot of commotion outside that went on and on and on. They got more and more concerned. Finally the doors were opened and they saw a great big party was laid out. The Indians couldn't tell them in English that they wanted them to stay, but they had understood that Blanche and Herb were on their honeymoon and this was a big celebration for the newlyweds!

Afterwards they continued on and eventually got to the West Coast. Herb began working. At this time the airplane was becoming very popular and airstrips were being installed all over the West. Herb's job was preparing the runways. They traveled all over the United States building these runways. The RV part comes in now because, since they were on the road, it was sensible to have their home travel with them. But in 1927 there weren't very many RVs so Herb built a trailer. Blanche said he did a terrific job and it had absolutely everything you could need, including a little wood-burning oven. During the next number of years they had three sons, who went to 136 different schools. The family traveled around the country going from airstrip to airstrip. During the war years, Herb's services were especially in demand.

When I met Herb and Blanche in 1987, they were in their mid-80s. Through the years they traveled continuously while they raised their three children. When they retired, they continued to travel. Unfortunately the three sons absolutely hated traveling. As soon as they became adults, they went to Victoria, British Columbia, stayed there and never traveled anywhere. But as Blanche said to me, "Three weeks in any one spot is more than enough for me." So she and Herb would leave Florida, travel slowly across country and get to Victoria about May. They'd leave their RV, visit with their children, and get on their sailboat to go to Alaska. In the fall, before the weather got really bad, they'd sail back down, leave the boat, get back in the RV, have a short visit in Victoria, and off they'd travel again to Florida.

Sixty years, still traveling, and still enjoying their life together. That must be a record.

*Ann Howell, born in England, has been a citizen of the United States since 1963. She and partner David have been full-timers since 1994. In addition to spending time with her three daughters and two grandsons, her favorite activities are reading, arts, crafts, theatre, movies, exploring restaurants, and traveling in the United States and abroad. Ann also contributed "Another Mouse."*

# *Exit Ramp*

## WHAT I WISH I HAD BROUGHT BUT DIDN'T:

- anything I didn't bring, I can buy, as long as it fits in the motorhome and doesn't add weight. *JL*

- I didn't miss a thing from my home. My kids said to say I missed them. I do, but they have their own lives. *BC*

- more patience to enjoy the process of travel rather than the destination. *DW*

- uh . . . I think I brought everything. *SE*

- my bike. *NA*

- I can't think of anything. *AF*

- my blender. Paul sold it before I had a chance to put it in the "take" pile. *SB*

- my dad. He's gone now, but, oh, how he would have enjoyed the RV lifestyle. *CT*

- more kitchen stuff like the blender and large casserole pan. We didn't think we would have enough room. *LE*

- a small, portable sewing machine. I got one after four years on the road. *JW*

- a big cooking pot. *CC*

- after eight years of full-time RVing, if I missed it, I replaced it! We are not deprived. *JA*

# Uniquely Women

- - - - - - - - - - - - - - - - - - - - - - - - - - - - - - - - - - - - - - - - - - - - - -

*When women take to the road, whether alone or with a partner, they face the same problems and challenges that they might off the road. Life goes on. In addition, it can be difficult to find women friends. In these stories, our writers share how they found women to talk to and have coped with issues close to their heart.*

*Women RVers often find themselves missing "women talk."*
*DeAnna found her community in an RV kitchen*
*(of course) one Hanukkah when a Jewish RVer*
*got everybody together to peel ten pounds*
*of potatoes for potato latkes.*

# Women's Friendships

DeAnna White

I GREW UP IN MIDWEST SAMENESS: PEOPLE OF THE SAME COLOR, the same religion, and the same farm background. Books were my only transportation to other cultures. I dreamed of seeing the world through eyes that had a different life experience than mine. In time I moved to the city, met a man, and fell in love. When I was thirty, life threw one of its magical curves. We had a serious accident and could no longer work. We received a settlement and the chance to start life anew. The images of the open road caught our imagination: soaking in hot springs, finding our own little isolated mountaintop, and spending a month snorkeling on our own beach in Mexico. We were filled with excitement when we bought our first RV to begin our new journey.

When we started traveling, I thought the journey was about seeing different parts of this continent, living in them, and learning about their rich cultures. The first two years of travel were times of delight and awe, living in places so different from Missouri. My honey and I were continually on the move, enjoying the intensity of all the new experiences. Yet I felt a loss; I missed my women friends. By grabbing on to this traveling life, I had left behind women who knew me. Now I connected with strangers in new places. "Where are you from, where are you going?" The getting acquainted dance played on and on. How do I connect with these strangers? Then we met up with some younger RVers at a Thanksgiving rally in Pena Blanca, Arizona. Some of us knew each other from previous gatherings and some had just started traveling. None of us realized that we were about to have a life-changing experience.

Of course it happened in a kitchen. Even on the road in our little travel boxes, we followed the ritual of getting acquainted by cooking. The challenge was finding a motorhome with enough seating so we all could participate. It was during Hanukkah and Alice was missing her Jewish community. She wanted to share her culture and suggested we all make *latkes*, traditional potato pancakes that even this non-Jewish group could cook. We collected an assortment of pots, Alice brought the ingredients, and Jaimie offered her motorhome. Somehow peeling potatoes in the kitchen gave us a way to share our lives.

I was struggling with a problem with my husband. We had traveled for a few years living in a 24-foot trailer. Al had decided he wanted to get a computer and get into surfing the Web. I felt he was leaving me and escaping into the computer. We had developed such an intimacy in our relationship. He was my best friend and sole companion twenty-four hours a day. I was feeling abandoned. Kay listened to my tale of woe and kindly suggested I get a hobby. A few hours on the computer was not going to be the end of the rich relationship my sweetie and I had developed. She said, "Get a grip, girl. A little time alone is a good thing." We laughed about it and she offered to teach me some of the basics of playing an electronic keyboard. She shared her stories and I realized how much we had in common.

As we peeled potatoes and drank tea, we talked about our lives beyond the superficial conversation of strangers. We talked of children, our loss of friendships with other women, and how we felt about traveling. The diversity of life experiences of this group of women astonished me, all with such rich stories to tell. They were ready to test their limits, try new physical challenges, explore their spirituality, and expand their creativity through writing, photography, and music. I heard stories of dealing with abandoned careers and the loss of that life. Some shared fears of illness ending the travel lifestyle. All of us were struggling to find meaning in our nomad lives. We shared the need of someone to hear our stories and understand.

When Gloria talked about how she missed being around people who knew her, we all felt the loss. None of us had developed a circle of women with whom we could share the intimacy of our life stories. In that tiny kitchen, a shift occurred and we began to talk of our lives. Beyond the basic cocktail conversation, we now shared bits of our passions. While I learned from Marie how you turned dried red peppers into a magical sauce for chips, she confided that she and her husband were torn between staying on the road and finding a place to settle. The sharing continued during the next four days, affecting us all. We were no longer strangers who only shared the RV lifestyle. We had shared a bit of who we were and a community of women's friendships began.

Looking back, I realize now that for me the journey is not about the places. For me it is the gift of peeking into other women's lives through their stories and finding the bonds that tie women's friendships.

*DeAnna White has lived on the road since 1983. She travels with her partner, Al Stovall, and her dog, Dusty. DeAnna also contributed "San Miguel de Allende."*

*After years of searching for her long-lost child, Donna stands at a pay phone in a remote desert town and hears her daughter's voice for the first time.*

# First Daughter

Donna Ellis

"START A NEW LIFE AND FORGET THIS EVER HAPPENED," WAS WHAT they told us all after we had our babies. It doesn't always work that way.

In 1960, at the age of sixteen, when I was a senior in high school, I had a baby girl in a home for unwed mothers. Having a child out of wedlock was a terrible stigma in those days, and I gave up the baby for adoption. I knew I could never raise her on my own, but I could never stop thinking about her.

I met my "now husband of forty years" a year later, and after I knew our relationship was a stable one, I wrote back to the home to see if she had been adopted. She had. I then tried to do what they suggested and live my life without guilt. We raised his two children from a previous marriage and had two together, but at times I would wonder if my first daughter was happy, if she was creative, well adjusted, or even alive.

In 1993, when we were first RVing, another couple came over to our motorhome for supper one night, and the wife of the couple was very excited. She was flying to Florida to meet her birth parents and siblings for the first time. When I saw her happiness, memories of my daughter came flooding back. It made me want to meet and know my own daughter, too.

I began my search for her. Luckily, my husband was supportive but all my efforts ended in dead ends. We had put notarized letters into all of her files, giving her our names and ways to contact us if she ever searched, but officials told us that she had never asked to open her files.

I finally decided that we had spent enough time, energy, and money and we had done all we could do. I could then only hope that she would one day search for ME. That's when I began to write my own history for her, so that if she didn't search until after I was dead, at least she would have everything I could remember about how she came to be and how I had tried to find her. I finished her book and my husband knew to save it for her if I died first.

Over the years, I had shared this event with a few close RV friends. All were supportive and encouraging but had no new ideas. Then, in the fall of 1998 an acquaintance introduced me to her "new" son, who had been adopted out as an infant like my daughter. I told her about my search for my daughter. She asked me if I had filled out the state's official form. I hadn't. She told me to write for it since that was how she had found her son.

My husband and I leave the Midwest in our RV every fall and head for winters in the Southwest where it's warm. The Kansas Adoptee's form didn't reach us in the mail until November. We filled it out, had it notarized, and put it back in the mail in December. I was afraid that this form would be like the other letters in her file—a dead end.

Less than a month later we were in Quartzsite, Arizona, for our annual gathering of RV friends. One sunny January day, my husband and I drove into town to get groceries. We stopped at the pay phone in front of the store to pick up our voice mail messages. The last message was a strange female voice, telling me her name and about her life. It took me a few minutes to realize who it was—my long-lost daughter! I began to laugh and cry at the same time.

The two of us talked many times on the telephone in the next several days. I had to meet her. I didn't want to wait until spring when we returned to the Midwest so we left our RV and drove all the way back there in the car to meet her and her family. I gave her the "book" which I had written, so she would know that she had never been forgotten, and we had a family gathering to welcome our "newest, oldest" member. Our family was now complete.

But that first day, when we returned to the RV gathering and told them I had had a call from my daughter, there wasn't a dry eye in the group. We all celebrated an end to my "missing piece," and, as I write this, three Januarys later, back here in the same place, I'm still so grateful for the chance to know my daughter and for my supportive family of RV friends.

*Donna Ellis' home has always been Independence, Missouri, until she and husband Al discovered the OTHER places on the road. She loves creativity and does beadwork for several galleries. Even though they still have a house, she considers herself a full-time RVer since that's where her heart is. Donna also contributed "The Whale" and "Most Beautiful Place."*

# I Wish I Could

Janice Lasko

I WISH I COULD
See like an eagle
Move my head like an owl
Run like a gazelle
Hear like a rhinoceros
Have the colors of a butterfly
Fly like a bird
Have the endurance of an elephant and
The strength of an ant.

But if all my wishes came true,
Who would I be?

*Janice Lasko also contributed "I'd Rather Walk" and several short pieces.*

*Friendship can come in many forms. As Phyllis moved*
*into the RV lifestyle, she discovered another*
*facet of connection to others.*

# Friends

- - - - - - - - - - - - - - - -

## Phyllis Frey

A FRIEND IS SOMEONE WHOM "ONE KNOWS WELL AND LIKES" according to my mini-Webster's Dictionary that doubles as a lap top computer stand when my trusty electronic device is sitting atop a small cocktail table in my RV. My faithful printer sits sideways on the little table and sort of hangs off the side a bit and covers the bottom part of the window behind the table, but not enough to block the view of the outside world. I lovingly refer to this rather low-tech set up as my computer desk. A little offbeat, but functional and comfortable, like an old friend. Webster goes on to say that to *like* means to "be fond of; to enjoy". Another quick definition from my little book brings us full circle. The word *fond* means "to like." Mr. Webster may be a man of many words but only uses very few of them at a time.

Before I hit the road as a full-time RVer, I worked as a nurse. I used to hang out a lot with my best friends from the hospital, and we would share common aspects of our lives. We went out to dinner and talked about the job, the problems with the kids, the bills, the boss, and rehash all the latest gossip. In fact, rehashing gossip may have been the most important aspect of the relationship. It provided an escape from the everyday trials of our own hectic lives and provided a sense of security and relief by reaffirming that we were not alone in our plight. Together we formed a herd of stressed out and unhappy people trying to figure out why we were like that.

We chased the American Dream until we were so caught up in it there seemed to be no escape. We got better jobs, raises, and promotions. We bought more stuff, moved to bigger houses, and took more exotic vacations. Faster and faster we chased that which eluded us until one day, head spinning out of control, I screamed, "Stop! Enough of this." It didn't take long after that to figure out that what I needed was not more, but less—much less of everything. I knew right then I wanted a big change.

As I evolved into a full-time traveler, my concept of "friend" has changed. I always believed the definition of a friend to be many-faceted and subject to my own personal interpretation. I now allow people to define themselves and their roles in relationships. I do not classify and put people in cubbyholes like I used to. I enter into a relationship with no preconceived notions or expectations. I have adopted a "wait and see and just enjoy in the meantime" attitude. I have not been disappointed in the five years we have been on the road. I've remained in contact with some of the friends from my traditional stick house and work days, but the relationships are different now. I find I have less in common with them, and I no longer enjoy the latest gossip. They move entirely too fast for me these days.

Of course, not every new relationship has worked out to become a lasting friendship. Some people have passed quickly through my life, and we have gone our separate ways. I am thankful for the short time they were in my life and what I learned from them. Even negative experiences have taught me important lessons. Others people have become important in my life, and I give thanks for them daily.

I am no longer intimidated by a culture that equates money with worth as a person. Nor am I intimidated by fluctuating social conditions or the recent economic ups and downs. Even though I seldom see many of my traveling friends, we stay in touch via phone, e-mail, and yes, even snail mail. Friendships continue to grow, and it is a joyous occasion when we are able to get together again to celebrate our lives and our lifestyle. We share a campfire and stories about our adventures as we contemplate the beauty of the night sky. We are thankful for each other. We have found the happiness in simplicity that eluded us in our old lives. We are a little offbeat, but we are functional and comfortable, like my dearly loved little computer desk—my old friend.

*Phyllis and her husband have been full-time RVers since 1997 when they sold or gave away everything anchoring them to a conventional house and lifestyle. After five years on the road, they feel too many adventures still wait around the next bend to ever return to the old life.*

*Men! Nan travels with her partner whom she dearly loves.*
*Unfortunately, he actually can stick to a low-fat diet*
*and never, ever, ever gossips. Sigh. She had*
*to find women friends.*

# In Search of
# A Good Haircut

-------------------------------------------------

## Nan Amann

WHEN I LEFT HOME FOR THIS NEW ADVENTURE, I WORRIED very little about the what-ifs. After all I was newly in love, a gypsy at heart, and didn't own enough stuff to make departure too much more than a big garage sale. I knew I would miss my daughters. I knew I would miss the snuggles and laughter of grandbabies. But that's why they made planes. "Have cell phone, will travel."

What I did not plan on was how much I would miss my heart friends. I waved gaily as we drove away. I'd had plenty of girlfriend time during the ten years of being single. Their lives were changing also as each of their families made different decisions about retiring. One had already started wintering in Colorado; another had bought a second home in Florida. One had taken the brazen step of becoming a flight attendant at fifty and was gone more than she was home. And one had made me totally jealous by hitting the road years before.

We had been through many changes together during the lifetime of our friendship, but we always knew we had each other. No one gets through this life unscathed, and each of us had sadness and had weathered almost unspeakable hardships. Like glue, we picked up each other's pieces and cemented the parts back together to go on. We could call on each other at any time for any reason and we would be there. We didn't even have to talk about the past. Or we could. Whatever the day or hour we held onto each other when needed. We had also laughed our way through many a tear.

I just did not realize how much women do for each other. A good friend, a truly good friend, will not let you buy something that makes your butt look big. A wonderful friend will let you vent and not remind you that eating chocolate will probably not solve the issue. An absolutely best friend will not repeat the awful things you say about the child/husband/brother/boss today. She won't even remind you later that you said it.

The man I live with is caring, loving, fun, and bright. He is, however, a man. He likes to solve rather than commiserate. He can actually stick to a low-fat diet. And he never, ever, ever gossips. Sigh.

Okay, I admit it. I have always adhered to the old adage, "If you don't have anything nice to say, come sit next to me." I had no idea I would miss female friendship so much. A girlfriend. A giggle. A little gossip. An appreciation for how tough it is to get a good haircut on the road. Have you noticed how seldom guys gossip? Is it because they don't notice? Don't care? Or do they just gossip when no women are around? I miss women. I miss chick flicks.

How do we find each other? How do we create truly great, close, loving friendships on the road? Without jobs, neighborhoods, schools, clubs or children to align us with other women with common interests, we must work hard at finding each other. Propinquity often helps us choose friends, a lucky accident of nearness. Strangely, common interests seem unnecessary. As runner or reader, birder or beader, Buddhist or Wiccan, knee-jerk liberal or that other thing, dreamer or doer, rock hound or couch potato, nudie or clotheshorse, we do have more in common than most. I appreciate beautiful beaded necklaces, but I am too much of a mess to attack little teeny beadwork. I admire a thin, lithe runner's energy, but oh the thought makes my knees ache. But be you wild child or momma's angel, we all share a love of star-studded skies and the howl of coyotes in the distance. We all share the wanderlust.

The nomadic lifestyle changes how you make friends. As my very first new friend on the road said, "If you are going to reach out to someone new for friendship, you must cut to the chase." We don't have time to pussyfoot around deciding whether or not we will be friends. To reach a deeper level of friendship, we have to scratch at the wounds that have healed over with time. We must share our stories, reaching back in memory to talk about the dysfunctional families, the losses suffered, the bad decisions we've made, the limbs we climbed out on. That is what begins to build the deep abiding sweetness that women create for each other.

I still miss my heart friends after almost two years on the road. But as each new dear friend is discovered, I feel so lucky to have found women who are open. Each enjoys new days, new roads, and new friends—and is also willing to tell me who cut her hair. Now that's friendship.

*Nan Amann was introduced to this lifestyle and to her life partner by her heart friends, Sue and Charles. She is an East Coast girl who was raised in a farming town in Minnesota, a definite flatlander. She loves chocolate, puzzles, blue jeans, opera, golf, tennis, wine, and Gothic smut. Nan also contributed "An Ode to Boondocking" and "Northern Minnesota."*

# Side Roads

### THE PEOPLE WE MEET BY JANICE LASKO

RVing to me is about the people we meet. There is a bond that brings RVers together no matter what their background was or is. There are no barriers. There also is a bond with people we meet along the way who don't RV, but are curious about how and why we live this lifestyle. They make me feel special in my daring to be different.

### SPECIAL PLACES BY CINDY COOK

The most special places are not memorable because of the fantastic rock formations, tall trees, crashing surf, or unique cacti. They are memorable because of the smiling faces of those who made me feel at home and, in some cases, did not want me to leave. Some of these folks took me to the heart of the place they live — a taste of local peanut butter pie, a tour of their woodworking shop, a drive to where they go to relax. These people are what have meant the most to me.

### CASUAL LIVING BY JEAN NELSON

We keep enough changes of clothing so we don't have to go to a Laundromat more than once a week. Since we don't go to places where we have to dress up, our clothes are casual, comfortable, and practical. Heavy, warm clothes for winter are stored. Propane for heating and cooking is much cheaper than gas. Electricity costs less than we used in our home.

*Sharing the grief of her daughter's death, Janet tells how traveling on the road became the bandage that covered her wounds to give her time to begin healing.*

# Kindred

Janet R. Wilder

WHILE RVING THROUGH ARIZONA IN 1991, I VISITED THE GRAND Canyon. Looking out over the rim, I realized that the time and forces that had created this wonder were so vast and ancient that my life, in comparison, was less than a speck of dust. In the schemes of Fate, Providence, Karma or what ever you choose to call it, I am inconsequential. Things happen. No one person is singled out by the powers that rule the universe. This realization reentered my consciousness several years later.

Two weeks before we were to begin our full-timing adventure, I lost my youngest child. Cara was renting a room near her college in order to take a summer course and an internship at a local business. She was twenty-one years old, about to begin her senior year at college, when an 86-year-old man, taking his 82-year-old sister to the doctor, lost control of his vehicle and hit Cara's car head-on. All three died instantly.

It was July 5, 1996, and the house in New Jersey was under contract-of-sale. All of our furniture had been sold. We still had the kitchen set, the refrigerator, and our bedroom set that were to be picked up in a week by the purchasers. We called them and requested an extra week. The rest of the house was empty. The funeral was on July 7. Neighbors and friends supplied folding tables and chairs for the one-week mourning period.

The new fifth wheel and truck sat in the driveway of our suburban New Jersey home.

On July 15, with all of the borrowed furnishings returned to their owners, I began to pack our remaining belongings into the fifth wheel. It was a Herculean task. After each trip to the trailer, I was so exhausted that I lay down on the floor, just inside the front door, to rest. I couldn't make it to the bedroom. I have always been a high-energy type. Stress evoked an extra jolt of adrenaline to my system and I rarely ran out of steam. This was different. The fatigue was overwhelming. It was paralyzing. Taking each step required every ounce of my strength.

Brief forays to the outside world for shopping or estate matters brought condolence wishes. Well-meaning as they were, they poked and probed at the fresh wounds of my grief. I began to avoid people I knew, turning a corner or an aisle, just so I didn't have to face them. I avoided taking in the mail in case a neighbor was outside. I couldn't bear to see my grief reflected in the eyes of those who knew Cara all of her short life.

Somehow, I managed to do what I had to, and we began our life as full-time RVers on July 22. I was excited, anxious and very, very fragile.

Traveling was a bandage that covered my wound. In the campgrounds no one knew me. Encounters with other human beings did not leave me in a heap of misery. I could talk to people without crying. I could rejoin the world of the living. We did some light sightseeing as I tired easily, but mostly I basked in the peace. There was no phone to ring. There was no daily mail with its cards and notes of condolence. Though the pain of my loss was always with me, I was able to briefly focus on other things. I took long walks. I watched the sunsets. I spent insomniac hours in a lawn chair, tracking the stars in their rotations. I chatted with fellow campers about our new status as full-timers and steered the conversations away from families. Slowly, by the hour, by the day, by the week, I began to heal.

RVers are capable of instant friendships because we spend so little time in one place. We are adept at trading travel tips, itineraries, and life histories in a few minutes. We hitch up and head out without commitment, happy to have shared each other's company for a little while. These encounters are the best part of RVing.

During our years of full-timing, I have met other women who've lost children. We may have only just met, but we hug, we cry, and we comfort each other. We have a need to share our grief with others who've been there. It makes us feel more normal and not so alone.

There is a small, informal RVing network of such mothers. When we first meet, some of us exchange e-mail addresses. When one of us learns of another RVer who has lost a child, she'll forward her e-mail address and those of us who can, write. We don't offer condolences. There are none. We are just there. When I am asked, "How do you go on," I answer, " There are no options."

I am not heroic. I am not strong. Losing my child has damaged me. I don't handle stress well anymore, and it's good that the full-timing lifestyle affords little. I recently lost my dad after a long illness. I couldn't grieve as I thought I should. He was eighty-one and had lived a full life. His last months were difficult and I know that he is in a better place, probably taking long walks with his beloved granddaughter, Cara, but I feel guilty about not grieving properly. I am grateful that no one in my RVing world knows who I used to be. They accept me as I currently am. The constant excuses to family and old friends are not needed here.

When asked, I tell new acquaintances that I have three children. I refuse to discount her as my child just because she is dead. I am not afraid to answer the question "Where do your children live?" I say "Two are in New Jersey, one is in Heaven."

Occasionally this response will evoke a tear in someone's eye and I will learn that she, too, has lost a child. Arms open wide. No matter how many years have gone by, the hug, like old-fashioned salve, draws out a drop of the lingering pain to be carried off with the wind. We are kindred. We have both traveled in the terrible place of heart-ripping grief. These fleeting, cleansing moments can only happen in a world of instant friendships, the world of the RVer.

*Janet R. Wilder, author of* Your Rolling Home: Housekeeping in an RV, *travels with her husband and their two mini-poodles. Janet also contributed "Moraine Lake" and "Well-traveled Dogs."*

*On construction jobs, most women find themselves relegated to cleaning and helping. Rebelling against removing bat droppings, Chris and her team formed the AAA Construction Company on a Habitat for Humanity build.*

# AAA Construction

## Chris Dishman

ONE OF THE BEST THINGS MY HUSBAND AND I DO FOR OURSELVES on the road is volunteer with the Habitat For Humanity RV Care-A-Vanners program. For two weeks at a time we work together with other RVers and members of a local community to build a house. During a two-week period our group can take a house from the foundation to being roofed and enclosed with windows and doors. Our favorite affiliate is located in Kellogg, Idaho. The area is called the Silver Valley because of all the silver mines that were located in the area. The folks there are incredibly supportive of our efforts. They provide lunches, snacks, sightseeing tours, and warm friendships.

Many people think that building a Habitat house is primarily a "guy thing." And, in truth, most men seem to be more comfortable wielding the tools of the building trades than women. However, at many of the Habitat builds there are also enthusiastic women who are learning to hammer and saw and drill. At the July 2001 Silver Valley build, there were several such women and one very knowledgeable construction supervisor, Verne.

On the first day of the build, Verne had each of us pair up with someone whom we did not know and had each two-person team tackle a job they were not familiar with. On the second day of the build he mixed up the teams and had each tackle some job other than the one they had had the day before. By the third day he was no longer pairing up people, but rather assigned individuals or groups to tasks from his various to-do lists. For the next couple of days, whenever we finished a chore and went to Verne, he would scratch his head, then consult his lists, and assign us a job.

Three of us ladies started to joke about the fact that we seemed to be getting the jobs that were on the "Z List." In other words, tasks that no one else would do or would want to do. For instance, one of the most odious jobs was cleaning bat droppings off some siding that had been stored in a field. Yuck! Following that job we approached Verne to tell him that we wanted to be assigned to one of the "A List" jobs instead of the "Z List" jobs. That was how we three all got assigned to build a door for the storage shed. Verne pointed to the pile of scrap material and showed us a similar door on another shed that we could use as a model. We looked at each other and started giggling. Two days later we hadn't stopped laughing, but we had a door that hung straight and worked fine. In the process we learned how to use a circular saw and a power drill, correct measuring techniques, and gained tons of self-confidence. We took a lot of ribbing from the other Care-A-Vanners because of all the laughter that emerged from the vicinity of the shed. We got dubbed the "AAA Construction Company" because the three of us had landed and completed a job from the "A List."

After our initial success, AAA Construction (Absolutely Awesome Accuracy) framed a couple of interior walls, cleaned debris from soffit pieces, and nailed up an OSB skirt strip to support the siding starter strip. Our last accomplishment, to the tune of much laughter, was to build shelves in the storage shed using metal studs and OSB.

We chatted and worked and laughed and worked and in the process made wonderful friendships. We appreciated being given real work and challenges to allow our skills to grow. We owe much of our success to Verne, who gave us the opportunities to show what we could do. Thanks to Habitat for Humanity and its RV Care-A-Vanner program for bringing us together.

*Chris Dishman, born in New Jersey, earned a B.A. from William Smith College in Geneva, New York. She has held a variety of jobs and at one time opened a needlepoint shop with her sister and mother. When the shop closed she became a computer programmer and analyst. Chris spent twenty-five years in the computer biz working for many Fortune 500 companies.*

*Using the big scale at the Publix market to track her weight loss,
Joanne learns that dieting does not mean only eating
half a bag of jelly beans instead of the whole one.
She finally keeps her New Year's resolution.*

# Losing Weight with Suzanne

Joanne Alexakis

AGAIN. I WAS READY TO TRY AGAIN. FOR THE LAST FIVE YEARS, my resolution for the New Year was drearily the same: To Lose Weight. Those resolutions were also frustrating in that they were forgotten before they were started. In spite of my track record, this January, my New Year's resolution was again—To Lose Weight.

I began the much-publicized Suzanne Somers' weight-loss program that included fruits, vegetables, proteins, fats, and some complex carbs. I was not a dieter so this was the first time I had ever used the term "complex carbs." The closest I had ever come to calorie counting and cutting back on food previously was last Easter, when I would eat only a half bag of licorice jellybeans at a time instead of the whole bag. So this was a big step, a turning point, a new way of living for me. My husband, Nick, was also on this regimen, because if he wanted anything else to dine on besides what Suzanne recommended, he would have to fix it himself. But like he said, "If you can't trust Suzanne Somers, who can you trust?"

The "eating plan" was really working! In six weeks I had lost fifteen pounds. However, I think just not consuming a half-dozen sugar cookies and three powdered-sugar doughnuts every morning helped too. There were some negative foods on this reducing program. For instance, I bought some of that prepackaged salad at the grocery store. The Fresh Garden Greens Style Salad consisted of lettuce, romaine, *frisée,* and carrots. Good healthy stuff. But my co-dieting spouse didn't like it; he said that it was like swallowing hair. And then I couldn't handle the three cold breakfast cereals that Somers recommended. Shredded Wheat tasted like earth, All-Bran tasted like earth also, and Grape Nuts tasted like earth with little stones in it. Give me Wheaties or Cheerios, please.

Since we were in sunny, tropical Florida, Nick and I enjoyed many delicious fruits. The mangos, kiwis, and exotic melons were fantastic. However, we both agreed that some foods were still not edible. For instance, Chinese pea pods were a foul-tasting disappointment. And chewing whole-grain pasta was like crunching on twigs.

It was obvious that reducing weight would take a while. After all, the dietary experts repeatedly stated, "It took a while to put it on." I claimed that it snuck up on me. Several years ago, I had quit smoking cigarettes. What a triumph! Well, I didn't really so much quit smoking as I had replaced that obsession with the "continuous-eating compulsion." As the pounds crept up, slimming down became a frequent wish.

When Nick and I began full-time RVing, an enlightening and meaningful new world opened up to us. My adventure-seeking mate and I enjoyed the road and traveling immensely. But being retired and taking it easy did not equate with staying physically active for us. I had never been an exercising person and luckily I had stayed medium-sized. In our other life, before beginning RVing, working at my job all day long had kept my body in motion and me away from food. However, by enjoying the relaxing RV lifestyle, I slowed down to sitting around a lot, grazing on munchies continually, and putting on the fat. My metabolism stalled.

I began exercising a little. I walked around the RV grounds every morning. Seven times around the perimeter of the park was about three miles. So, around and around I went, striding fast and hard. Of course, the month of July in Ocala, Florida, was horribly hot and the air was heavy with humidity. I sweated and wheezed and sweated some more. The poundage came off. After about six weeks, I reached a plateau in my weight loss. I started doing some short running spurts, making the pace more intense (walk, sprint, pant, pant, walk, run, huff, puff, plod, stumble, gasp, cough—you get the idea). As I cruised along, I carried two small one-pound dumbbells that I swung around to exercise my arms somewhat. My goal was to be muscle-bound.

We do not have a bathroom scale in our rig, so I used the big scale at the Publix grocery store to weigh myself. Each time I got on that scale and the needle pointed to even eight ounces less than the week before, I would cast my eyes heavenward and whisper, "Thank You, God, for helping me to take more blubber off this old carcass of mine."

Carol, my next-door neighbor at the trailer park, had been watching me hoof it around our RV community each morning. She said, "Boy, you've really lost the inches! I can see your clothes are just hanging off of you." I was so delighted and relieved to hear that someone else beside myself had noticed that the pounds were slipping off. I had shed twenty-five of them. I practically kissed her.

I went to Wal-Mart to buy new clothing. Nothing different—I was comfortable with my shorts and sleeveless blouses—just one size smaller. It was a joyous purchase. Also, my over-inflated ego let me buy a sexy pair of blue jeans at the JC Penney store in the mall. By the time I received my Penney's credit card bill for those denim pants, they no longer fit — they were too big! It was amazing, it was wonderful, it was expensive! So, I found a secondhand store, Second Chance, to sell my old (or maybe not-so-old) big clothes. I also bought my new smaller clothes from used-a-bit shops.

Friends asked me, "Don't you feel better, healthier, now that you have lost that extra weight?" My answer was, "No, not really." Fortunately, I had felt pretty darn good, even if quite bulky, before beginning the diet. But I was very proud of my progress. Tickled pink, actually. There was one negative, however. Fruit and flatulence. I once read where a gorgeous British model advised women to never eat any fruit because, "it gives you bloat." We all know what she meant by that and she was right. Following Suzanne Somers' suggestion, I tried to have my fruit servings an hour apart from other foods and it seemed to separate the fruit from its gastric outcomes. I was a lot more pleasant to be around.

Later that autumn, when Nick and I were in Tallahassee, Florida, another Escapees RV Club member moved into our park. We became daily walking buddies. Pat and I encouraged each other to gait faster and farther. We increased the size of our little dumbbells to two- and three-pounders. I even carried both of these dumbbells in one hand in order to be hefting five pounds at a time. Pat had a stopwatch to time our running sprints. We increased our endurance. We could move at a good trot for five minutes straight—whew! wow! whew-y! We performed warm-up and cool-down stretches using our RV-site picnic tables for exercise benches.

Since Pat and I footed it for an hour or more each session, I purchased a pedometer at Wal-Mart to measure the distance we covered. When my neighbor next door asked how far we ran each day, I told her that we weren't sure since we hadn't figured out how to set the device yet. She said that she had three pedometers just like that.

My thighs started to get muscled from my daily walking and jogging. It was a new me. However, there was still a lot of flab to be worn off those aforementioned thighs (and those hips and that behind) so the old me was still there, too. You could call me a well-rounded person, for sure! Nick called me "a hulk," but I believe he was just stroking my ego.

I was definitely pleased with my diet and exercise results. I had lost forty pounds. Finally a New Year's resolution was a success! Maybe next year, I will try another New Year's resolution: To Quit Forwarding E-mail Jokes. (*Editor's note: She did and I miss them!*)


*Joanne Alexakis is intrigued by living things—humans, plants, and animals. She was an optician for twenty years in Minnesota. She and husband Nick have been full-time RVers since April 1994. They work at state parks and RV campgrounds in cool northern United States in the summer and in the warmer South in winter. Joanne also contributed "Black Hills of South Dakota."*

*For many RVers, the journey is about roads traveled and beautiful places. For Mary, the essence of her journey is self-discovery*

# On Becoming a Golden Goddess

Mary Schaal

WE'VE ALL SEEN THE ADS: "GO RVING . . . LIFE'S A TRIP." THE WOMEN are attractive, fit, and smiling. They obviously weren't boondocking in an RV like mine, grooming with less than a gallon of water a day. Nor were they just returning from the Laundromat with a pile of clothes resembling the Leaning Tower of Pisa.

Don't get me wrong. I wouldn't trade living full-time in an RV for anything. Life IS a trip. It's just that mine has been a trip down a detour so curvy and steep that we pulled over to let bicyclists pass us on the way down.

When we left our "normal" life behind and hit the road, it felt like an extended vacation. We went where and when we wanted, propelled by whim and saved-up dreams accumulated during years of hard work. We had no lasting routines, schedules, or pressing engagements. Fiscal discipline gave way to impulse buying, and unplanned expenses mounted up. Cooking and shopping revolved around what was easy, fast, and available. And without regular exercise, my weight increased almost as fast as our debts. I began feeling "fat" about the same time my identity, formerly tied to my job, was being challenged. I wasn't particularly skilled as a navigator or a wife, though I was suddenly learning a lot about being in rather close quarters with a husband who long ago taught map-reading to Marines. My fear of being less than perfect became such a sore spot that I was defensive, irritable, and withdrawn. Even my spiritual devotion lagged as I felt more isolated and alone the farther we traveled from our former home. I had gone from being part of a community to complete solitude without peace.

In my newly adopted "Let life take its own course" attitude, I had become so passive that I had let my "self" silently fade away. I had a quiet crisis on my hands that took me a while to unravel. I didn't want to revert to my former ways of trying to control everything, but wasn't comfortable with becoming so laid back that I needed to check for a pulse to verify my own existence. I needed to learn a new lifestyle that was neither controlling nor passive. To me, this is what living the RV lifestyle has become. The real journey has been one of self-discovery.

I have been pleasantly surprised by what I am finding along the way. Although my sense of isolation lessened when I began to listen to myself, relate better to my husband, and reopen the lines of communication with God, my loneliness was cured when we accidentally found the Boomers group of the Escapees RV Club. We learned from women and men with a myriad of different experiences to share. Among them were a few kindred spirits who became close friends. Now, whether in touch by e-mail or in person, I am part of a community of travelers.

My husband and I also faced reality. Our overspending was stressing me out for a reason: I didn't want to return to year-round work. We made a budget and a plan to pay off our debts and found work amid our travels. We are so much happier, even though we give more thought to economy than we used to and plan our travels around seasonal work.

My poor diet and exercise were another example of self-discovery. The extra weight was making an arthritic foot hurt worse. And though dieting and exercising are hard, I realized that not doing so would be harder and harder on my health. I asked around among my friends and found a diet I could live with. I found a book with an exercise routine that would work in my mobile lifestyle. If I were in a painting today, I would still look more like a Rubens' than a Botticelli's "Venus," but over time, less paint will be required. The real point isn't about appearance, but by addressing my bigger concerns, I now have more energy and creativity left for life. I feel better because I am listening to myself and giving myself what I need.

Since hitting the road , I have learned first and foremost to laugh at myself and enjoy the journey, no matter how steep and curvy the detours. The views from such unanticipated routes are often surprising and noteworthy. Life is too short to live divorced from feelings, dreams, truth, and a sense of humor. I sincerely doubt that I will ever be featured as a skinny golden goddess in the "Go RVing" ads, but I affirm their message. I have learned that by following my authentic life path, I will eventually end up where I need to be.

*Mary Schaal and her husband Bob began traveling full-time in their motorhome in October 2000. An avid sport-kite flyer, dog lover, and boondocker, Mary finds renewal in the beauty of the ever-changing landscape and her simple lifestyle. She has a bachelor's degree from the Institute for Biblical Studies, Seattle. Mary also contributed "Pismo Beach" and "Scariest Moment."*

# Scenic Overlooks

## GOLDEN MOMENTS BY DARLENE MILLER

I am searching for gold
  under the Arizona sun.

I found
  a bullet jacket
    some square nails
      a piece of barbed wire
        a fractured geode
          no gold.

I also found
  a piece of blue sky
    through a hole in the mountain.

## SINGING WIND BOOKSHOP BY BARBARA CORMACK

My special place is in Benson, Arizona, called the Singing Wind Bookshop. Owned by Winifred Bundy, it is located about one mile north of Benson on a huge ranch. The bookstore is in the main house. We went on a day when they were having an afternoon of Cowboy Poetry readings, held in a glassed-in porch of the main house with a wood fire burning. We sat in the porch, hot soup and other delicious treats available, watching the wind blowing in the trees, the birds and wildlife just outside. A dusty black cat roamed among us. We spent the afternoon listening to artists playing their guitars and singing about the West and the hardships in those days. The sad stories and the hilarious ones were interwoven. For a day that started out with nothing planned, visiting the Singing Wind Bookshop was one of my favorites.

*Illness on the road has its particular challenges. Ardith describes how she and her husband dealt with cancer.*

# The Big "C"

---

## Ardith Fenton

*I'm sorry to say so but, sadly, it's true*
*That Bang-ups and Hang-ups can happen to you.*
DR. SEUSS

EVERY YEAR I GO FOR MY ANNUAL MAMMOGRAM, BUT I REALLY never expected to be diagnosed with breast cancer. When I received a message asking me to come in to have more images taken, I wasn't overly concerned.

The technician said "Don't worry, it's probably nothing." She took the images, but told me not to get dressed as she wanted them read before I departed. I waited, and waited, and waited. Finally, she returned to tell me that I could get dressed, but the radiologist wanted to speak with me. I quickly dressed. I told myself things would be okay. I had read the breast cancer risk list. I wasn't high risk.

The radiologist had the images on the screen. "What am I looking for?" I asked. I couldn't see anything that looked like a lump.

"See those white specks. Those are micro calcifications. In a breast they can indicate cancer," he responded. It looked like someone had sprinkled salt in a small area. "We need to do a biopsy to see why those calcium deposits are there. Do you have a surgeon?" he asked.

"No," I said.

He recommended Dr. Bagley, who was in the hospital. Ten minutes later, Dr. Bagley was sitting with me looking at my X-rays. He agreed that a biopsy should be done to determine if there was any cancer. "We can't do the biopsy today, but how about first thing Monday?" he suggested.

I saw him again in his office at four o'clock that afternoon. It would be an outpatient procedure. His last words were that 95 percent of calcium deposits are not cancer, so not to worry.

When I told Page, he was really worried. The big "C" word is so intimidating. Just the possibility that I might have cancer was frightening.

Eight o'clock Monday morning we arrived at the ambulatory care unit. The nurse who prepped and assisted kept my mind occupied with her questions about camping and our RVing lifestyle as Dr. Bagley did the procedure. He told me to call his office late Tuesday afternoon for the results. He seemed to understand how difficult it would be to wait for an answer.

It was awful to see and hear the fear in the faces and voices of my family. I reassured them the test would be negative. I was sure that we would be on our way to Alaska in a few days.

At six o'clock Tuesday night Dr. Bagley called. I knew that he was going to tell me there was no cancer. He said. "The bad news is you have breast cancer. The good news is that the cancer cells are still inside the mammary tubes."

I was paralyzed. It just couldn't be!

"We need to take more tissue so we can get a circumference free of cancer cells," he said. "I want to see you in my office Thursday."

I cried and cried. All I could think of was why now when we were doing just what we had always dreamed of doing. We exercised, our diet was nutritious, our stress was minimal, and we were happier than we had ever been. We had such plans.

Soon, I would wake up from this bad dream. But I didn't. We had to face the fact that I had cancer. I just wanted to be rid of this thing that had invaded my body. I had never considered my breasts of major importance to who I am. Would I feel incomplete or disfigured? How would Page feel? Would he be able to look at me the same? Was I going to die? Would I have chemo and lose my hair? We talked and talked and talked. Page just wanted me alive and healthy. We held each other and prayed.

Dr. Bagley explained our options. I could have a lumpectomy followed by six weeks of daily radiation. Three percent of the cancers aren't stopped with the radiation so they come back.

"What about a complete mastectomy?" we asked. That would mean removing the whole breast and some lymph nodes to be checked for any cancer cells that might have spread. There would be no need for radiation if the perimeter was clean and lymph nodes unaffected.

On Monday morning, just one week after the biopsy, I had a complete mastectomy. I was released the next morning with two drains. Page learned to empty and measure the drainage. With his supportive care my recovery was swift. By the third day, I was able to put my arm over my head to wash my hair. My sister called every day and sent pretty pajamas and inspirational readings.

Seven days after the surgery when the drains were removed, we got the Good News! The perimeter was clear and the lymph nodes unaffected. Dr. Bagley declared, "You had cancer. You do not have cancer."

"When can I travel?"

"Have you got your bags packed?"

"Yes."

"How about tomorrow?"

He indicated that the sooner I was on the road the better. The physical recovery would take a few weeks. The emotional healing would take a year or more, and the best way to start that healing was for us to get back in our fifth wheel and go on with our life.

My mastectomy was on April third. We were on the road to Alaska on April thirteenth. Since the Alaska Highway is rough in places, I hugged a pillow much of the way. At first, I thought people could tell by looking at me that I had had cancer. But during that summer there were times that even I forgot that I had only one breast. When I get frustrated with the prosthetic breast or comment on being disfigured, Page assures me that he is just glad to have me alive and well. His words are, "You are still you and I love you."

In the words of Dr. Seuss:
*You'll come down from the Lurch with an unpleasant bump.*
*And the chances are, then, that you'll be in a Slump.*
*And when you're in a Slump, you're not in for much fun.*
*Un-slumping yourself is not easily done.*

Well we did un-slump ourselves and created our own poem:
*We're off to Great Places!*
*Today is our day!*
*Our mountain is waiting.*
*We're on our way!*


*Ardith Fenton and husband Page still own, though no longer operate, a 500-acre dairy and maple farm in Vermont. They've been on the road five years. Traveling in a 31-foot Teton fifth wheel, they've worked on a farm in North Dakota, at an RV dealership in Anchorage, Alaska, and spend winters in Wilmington, North Carolina.*

# Ode to Boondocking

Nan Amann

"I REALLY DON'T MIND IF YOU DON'T SHAVE YOUR LEGS.
Just don't use much water!" he pleads and he begs.
He can shower completely in less than a minute
Using less water than I need to make tea in it.
"Cold water's invigorating!" He pronounces with glee.
"Just try it, you'll like it!"  (It's his fantasy.)
Using solar hot water from a bag that he's hung
I prance naked trying to remove all the scum.
"He's worth it," I mumble.
"No problem!" I say.

He claims we can boondock for weeks at a time
On just forty gallons of water—not forty of wine.
But I'm from the world of two flushes, you see
The first for noise cover, and the second for—well you know.
I dream of hot steamy baths with white soapy suds
Of soaking my feet as well as my duds.
I remember dishwashers! I could go on and on.
Now I listen to black water talks with a yawn.
"He's worth it," I mumble.
"No problem!" I say.

No matter I love him in spite of the smell.
There is one immutable fact I must tell.
Without a hot shower, I get mean and cranky.
Without a hot shower, there's no hanky-panky.


*Nan Amann also contributed "In Search of a Good Haircut" and "Northern Minnesota."*

# *Exit Ramp*

## THE BIGGEST CHANGE IN ME SINCE I'VE BEEN ON THE ROAD IS . . .

✍ learning to live with myself and enjoy my own company. *BC*

✍ my friendship with my husband. The road's isolation creates an intense bond of trust and we depend on each other. *DW*

✍ living in the moment, letting go of worry, and not trying to control everything. *MS*

✍ I am utterly and completely relaxed, lazy, and useless. I love it. *NA*

✍ my faith in God has taken over. I give each day to Him and know that all will be okay. *AF*

✍ I am more outgoing. *SB*

✍ my literally stopping to smell the roses. *CT*

✍ the independence and realizing there are so many possibilities that I wouldn't have thought of before, for work and play. *LE*

✍ I have come to think of time, which used to be my enemy, as my friend. The second biggest change is the fifteen pounds I've accumulated over six years. *JW*

✍ I need less "stuff"(except Beads!) *DE*

✍ I'm more creative and appreciate time even more. *CC*

✍ being relaxed. *DS*

✍ I've gained confidence. *JA*

# Encounters

------------------------------

*Sometimes a day starts out as ordinary but turns out to be extraordinary. Whether by chance or design, encounters add spice to our travels. Our writers remember and share encounters—delightful, fearful, intriguing—that are special to them.*

*The past is usually past, but for Lisa and Bryce, it lingered on in frequent chance encounters.*

# Close Encounters— or Let's Finish This Karma, Already!

Lisa Jackson

THE DIVORCE, SOMETHING I NEVER THOUGHT WOULD HAPPEN to me, did indeed happen in 1985, ending a twenty-eight-year marriage. I will spare you the whys and wherefores. It was over rapidly, or as rapidly as the state would allow; we survived and "went on with our lives," both remarrying, he the day after the divorce was final, Bryce and I some months later.

For the next several years we had no contact with "John and Marsha" (names have been changed, blah, blah), even though we lived in the same community. Then, in 1989, another lifestyle change: Bryce and I became full-timers at the same time, as happenstance would have it, they also took to the road. Oh, yes, and we both joined the Escapees RV club unbeknownst to each other. It was not long after that, that the unplanned, unpredictable, strange encounters began.

All RVers end up at Quartzsite, Arizona, in January sooner or later where it seems like millions of people are EVERYWHERE in those four corners of the desert. So what are the chances of meeting them? Bizillion to one? There I am, minding my own business, browsing down "J" lane at Tyson Wells when I walk right into, you guessed it, John and Marsha. No SKP hugs here, but constrained politeness all 'round.

Maybe this second one isn't quite so odd since it was a small town where we were attending an Escapade, and we do have eating in common, but there was more than one restaurant. Nonetheless, we were with a number of friends, just beginning our meal, when who walks by our table? You guessed it—John and Marsha.

Next was the community Thanksgiving dinner we were invited to share with friends in the center at Jojoba Hills Escapees park. It looked like it was going to be a full house, and the tables for eight were filling up fast. Ours had two seats remaining, the only seats vacant when "they" arrived late. J and M sat down before they realized we were there—and yes, they stayed.

Now, who could have predicted this one? As we were lugging our big fifth wheel west on the very busy 210 freeway outside of Los Angeles, a vehicle starts passing us and honking. RVers out there know this usually means there's a problem with the rig. The last time this happened to us, our bikes had fallen off onto the freeway. Apprehensively, we looked out expecting at the very least to see a trail of leaking holding tanks, but no, just John and Marsha again, waving as they passed us.

During this same period, Bryce and I were working for AGS, the RV park map guide company, and were doing a stint at the Pomona, California, Fairplex, soliciting ads that would support their Visitor's Guide. We were staying in the RV park and working out of the office there. Late one morning I was just leaving said office when what to my wondering eyes should appear? Yes, John and Marsha to check in for a week's stay. At least their site wasn't next to ours.

I have saved the best for last, although in my fading memory it was the first of these "accidents." Since Roseburg 1990 was our first Escapade, it seemed important to us as new SKPs to do everything "right." The first night we had been out to dinner with friends, taking longer than we'd planned and arrived late at the evening's opening meeting. The place was packed. We looked around for seats. The only ones we could see were at a picnic table far in the back. Heads down and locked, trying not to attract attention, we aimed for that table. Believe me when I say this, I did not know until I sat down that I was sitting right next to, oh yes, that very same duo. To this day, I'm convinced they believe I did it on purpose. Maybe, on some level, I did.

These odd synchronicities occurred over a period of years, roughly 1990-94, then just as strangely as they began, they ceased. Perhaps I'm just a slow learner, or perhaps it took me longer than most to adjust to the enormous changes in my life, but whatever the reasons, I can now feel the transition from that past life to the new one is complete—but what an interesting one it was!

*In her "past life" Lisa Jackson, originally from New York, was an RN, an Air Force wife, and lived in many places before settling in California in 1968 and raising four children. Now she and Bryce, still RVers and living in a motorhome with their two cats, spend much time in Southern California near their ten grandchildren.*

*Sometimes a special moment comes to us like a gift. In Newfoundland, Donna experienced such a moment when a Beluga whale looked right into her eyes.*

# The Whale

Donna Ellis

RVING BRINGS MANY WONDERFUL EXPERIENCES, BUT A QUITE recent experience was one of my most thrilling. My husband Al and I spent the summer exploring the Canadian Maritimes, a trip we had wanted to make for years.

In August, we found ourselves on the northwestern coast of Newfoundland near the town of St. Anthony. The local people who ran the RV park told us to go to Goose Cove, a small fishing village not too far away, if we'd like to see a whale. Wow! We dropped our plans for that day, grabbed our binoculars and camera, and drove there immediately. It was a gray, cool day and the tiny village was but a crescent surrounding the large cove. We found a place to park the car off the road, where we could see the entire cove. And there we sat for quite a long while, one or the other of us scanning the waters with the binoculars, looking for that telltale spout, but nothing. Finally, we gave it up and spent the remainder of the day sightseeing, so all was not lost.

The following morning, the same local couple asked us if we had gotten to see the whale, and we told them what we had done. They very excitedly explained that you had to just drive down to the dock and get out of your car and walk down to see it up close. Naturally, we scrapped our sightseeing for that day and drove straight there. As we neared the dock, there she was, a small female Beluga whale. The fisherman said he had caught her in his net by mistake three years before, and she had been returning to Goose Cove every summer. When I asked him what would happen when it began to get cold, he told me that she left each fall and returned in the spring. There were two children below the dock, sitting in his small boat, petting the whale. She obviously liked it, for she would stay right there as long as someone would pat or stroke her.

After I had taken many photos with my digital camera, the fisherman asked if I could take his photo with the whale. I not only snapped a bunch, but presented him with his own disk full of photos. He then invited ME to go down into his boat and pet the whale. At first it just felt like too much and initially I declined, but within a few seconds I was thinking, "Stupid—when will you ever get this opportunity again?"

Husband Al took the camera while I descended the old wooden ladder into the boat. I reached down to feel the smooth, cool, gray body in the water with tears streaming down my face. Even now, months later, I can't think of this event without tears of happiness. I spent some minutes just patting and stroking her back, when she suddenly turned in the water and *looked right into my eyes*. As I recall, her eye was a brilliant orange color, but the color wasn't important. I felt like she could see into my soul. All the past became nothing and only the moment was electric. It felt as though I had been struck by lightning, except that my heart felt an immense calm and so much gratitude for getting to experience this moment in time. It was, indeed, an experience never to be forgotten.


*Donna Ellis also contributed "First Daughter" and "Most Beautiful Place."*

# Animal Crossing

### THE MOUSE BY BARBARA CORMACK

In a campground in the middle of nowhere, it's five o'clock and nature calls. I sleep in the altogether and open the cupboard and see a tiny little mouse chewing up my toilet paper. What would you do? Put something on or grab a towel? I grabbed a towel, as I knew the mouse wouldn't be there after I dressed. Decision—how do I put on my housecoat and hold the mouse? Here I am with towel and mouse in one hand and holding my housecoat in the other and looking at my door to the outside world, laughing my head off. I got the door open and threw out the mouse and went back to bed. Someone said, "Why put on a housecoat when it was dark?" Well, with my luck someone would have been out walking.

### ANOTHER MOUSE BY ANN HOWELL

We're in bed in the old rig and all of a sudden we hear some water running and then stop, then start again in the toilet. "What is it?" we asked each other since we were both together and shouldn't have heard anything. David gets up to look inside the toilet. Sitting inside the bowl is a little mouse, who is jumping up trying to get out. Every time he fell down again he would land on the valve that shifted just enough to let a trickle of water escape, thus explaining the sound we were hearing. Of course, I also asked myself, "Was he there when I did my final toilet run before bed?" And would he be telling his grandchildren in the future, "Watch out for the waterfall in that rig."

The next question is "What do we do?" My initial reaction is "Flush it!" But we decided that if David would put his glove on, he could reach in and get him out. Which he did. But now what do we do with him? So he opened the door and threw him as far as he could.

We get back into bed and we're lying there. It was only a matter of minutes before the mouse was back in the rig. We couldn't believe it. Ah, life on the road.

*After arriving in a Baja campground, Myrna meets her neighbor,*
*a tall, bronze, loud, tough-looking woman with a mean dog*
*and a stormy marriage. First she was intimidated.*
*Then she became fascinated.*

# Baja Babe

- - - - - - - - - - - - - - - - - - - - - - -

## Myrna Courtney

THE FIRST TIME I SAW BAJA BABE I WAS A TAD MORE THAN
nervous, just looking at her. We pulled our fifth wheel into a crowded
beach campground, and Babe and her husband had pegged out a tent in
the next lot. Tall, bronze, lean, and tough, in cutoffs and a halter top, her
long raven-black hair tied back with a headband, Babe stepped out of
that tent like a gorgeous Amazon. She slapped the sand off of her pants
and yelled at their lean mean dog lunging on a chain. Then she yelled at
her husband to yell at the dog, and then she turned those sharp dark eyes
on us. I swear I was trembling. She never said a word, just peered at us for
a minute and then went back in the tent and kicked her husband out,
and when I saw him, I did tremble. He was big as a mule with a red beard
and—honest—little beady eyes, and I never saw him again without some
kind of drink in his hand. Very quietly I said to my husband, *hey, let's get*
*another spot* and he said *are you kidding I just spent twenty minutes getting*
*this rig in this tight spot and besides there aren't any more spots let's go get some*
*tamales up at the cantina.*

I gave Babe and her husband a wide berth for the next couple of
weeks, a thing that wasn't that easy due to their propensity for quarrels at

two in the morning, the decibel count of their most ordinary conversations, and the lean mean dog lunging on the chain. One night she nailed her husband on the head with a huarache. Another night he stormed out of the tent and fell asleep on the sand two inches from my bedroom window. I did manage a conversation or two, however, and honestly I found myself becoming utterly fascinated with the two of them. They borrowed the electric outlet in the side of our rig, brought over a lug of fresh strawberries, invited the whole campground over for the shared price of a bottle of rum, and whipped up the most incredible strawberry daiquiris we ever had. And one night around the campfire Babe's husband, who had a wonderful intelligence underneath the beard and the belly and the beer, told a story about touching a whale's tongue and you know, I believe he really has touched a whale's tongue. And Babe spent summers cooking on a salmon boat, which has to be something Jack London would think twice about. They were like that.

Babe scowled and strode about and shot off loud remarks that made me think of a grade-school bully who once threatened to beat me up after school for throwing the kick-ball too hard at her. They lived on the beach all summer with little but the tent and a few belongings on pegs, while I had a virtual mansion on wheels next to her, and I saw in her slightly mocking eyes what she thought of my suburban comforts.

Then my husband had an unfortunate encounter with a broken sidewalk in town and ended up in a cast. For the next week or two I had to drive the Gut Wrencher, our two-ton diesel International. The Mexican men stepped off the sidewalks to watch me drive by and shook their heads in amazement at the sight of the Gringo woman driving that big truck while her husband sat next to her doing nothing about it.

I pulled the truck into our site and there stood Baja Babe, hands on hips, the Gulf wind whipping that black hair around her beautiful face, scowling as usual. I felt the familiar intimidated twinge for a second, and just caught myself from pulling the truck to the other side of the rig. When I climbed down Babe saw it was me who had been driving, and suddenly she strode straight for me. My husband says I jumped back, but really, now. Then Baja Babe stuck her hand out and grabbed mine, pumping up and down in the strongest handshake I have felt before or since, from man or woman either one.

"Al-right!" she shouted as I stood there frozen, my arm flaying about wildly in her grasp. She threw an arm around my shoulder with such force it snapped my jaws shut. "Any woman that can drive that big ol' truck and not just stand around and let her man do all the heavy work for her is al-right!" And she shouted for her husband to bring me a daiquiri and to make the lean mean dog on the chain shut up.

I know it sounds like that song, but me and Baja Babe sat around the campfire until two in the morning that night, and she told me about her mother and I told her about mine, and we sang every '50s song we knew more than the first line to, and the lean mean dog stopped lunging and dozed with his head on my foot all night, and Baja Babe said I was al-right a few more times.

I can't remember having such a good time on a Baja beach.

*Myrna Courtney, a writer, has been RVing with her husband, who is a photographer, for thirty years. Throughout that time she has shared her travel experiences in RV travel magazines and other publications. They live in Grass Valley, California, when not traveling in the United States, Mexico, Canada, and Europe. Myrna also contributed "Woodstock, Vermont."*

*An encounter with a lonely marker at the top of a mountain sparked Kay's interest to uncover the story behind it: a man who had lived and died for his principles.*

# The House on Francis Mountain

Kay Peterson

THERE ONCE LIVED A MAN WHO CARRIED A HOUSE TO THE top of a mountain.

My husband and I were exploring one of the many trails that criss-cross the Arizona desert when we discovered a path meticulously lined with rocks that led up the side of a mountain to a ridge overlooking the towns of Oracle and San Manuel. Each tree was painstakingly circled with a rock border to capture the sparse rainfall and keep the trees from dying. A handmade bird feeder stood as a silent, undeniable testimonial that once someone had lived here. Yet, we could not find even one rotting piece of lumber.

Then we saw it. Not the remnants of the homestead we were look-ing for, but a stone marker on a concrete pedestal. At the foot of the marker sat a man's boot daring the elements to destroy that one small trace of human existence. A copper shield attached to the front of the marker had barely legible words scratched on it. "Earl Francis built his home here. The Government forced him to vacate both house and min-ing claim. In answer, he sat on two boxes of dynamite and lit a match."

Why was a house so important that a man would kill himself? And how did the house disappear without a trace? When we returned to the ranch where our trailer was parked, we learned that we had been on Francis Mountain. It isn't the official name, of course. Earl was a small man, only five feet five and weighed barely 135 pounds. When he died at the age of thirty-five, the one thing everyone remembered most about him was his big smile underscored by Lincoln-like chin whiskers. He was born in Washington, D.C. and hated the congestion of city life. So in 1953, at the age of twenty-two, he headed west on a small motorcycle. By the time he reached the Tucson area, he was out of money. He would remain here for the last thirteen years of his life.

When Congress passed the Mining Act of 1872 to hasten the growth of the West, the elusive promise of gold drew many prospectors. The difference between the others and Earl was that Earl was seeking freedom. When he found some gold deposits and registered his claim, the Government was still encouraging prospectors to build homes on the land near their claims.

Since there was no road up the side of the mountain where Earl established his claim, he had to carry all the building materials on his back. His small frame was often bent double under the weight of sacks of cement and lumber.

It took a year to build a sturdy stone house with glass picture windows and all the comforts, including lights from a gasoline-powered generator and running water from a tank on his roof with pipes leading to the kitchen and bathroom. When there was no rain to fill his tank, he hauled water in a bucket from a spring at the bottom of the mountain. The entire house cost $500 to build. Earl, an amateur painter, filled the house with his own paintings, mostly of sunsets.

He worked his mine in the old way, digging a shaft eight feet deep, smashing the rock with a hammer, and sifting to find the minute particles of gold. Once a month he took the gold into town where he traded it for a few dollars. When the district ranger learned of Earl's house, he told Earl he would have to tear it down because his claim was not producing enough gold to justify a prudent and reasonable man investing his resources in the hope of a profit. A claim was only valid if the mine was a profitable venture. Earl argued. "All I need is $30 a month for living expenses."

During the long months of waiting for a court decision, Earl's love of the desert deepened, the way something we truly care about so often does when we fear we will lose it. When his friends asked what he would do if he lost, he said, "I don't know, but I can never go back to working eight hours a day for any man. That's the worst thing a man can do." Earl didn't hire a lawyer. He believed in justice. The court would honor his claim. He was wrong.

After many months, after pages of reports and hours of testimony by mining experts, the Court denied his claim. He appealed. On August 15, 1966, he went to the post office to pick up his mail. There it was further stipulated that if he did not voluntarily tear down his house, a bulldozer would be brought in "to restore the land to its natural state." With shoulders hunched in defeat, he turned and walked into the desert. Later that afternoon, he walked to the home of his closest friends. With him was his sole companion, a shaggy-haired dog with the ridiculous name Cadillac. Earl asked if they would take care of his dog. He had business to attend to.

Hours later, at 5:30 p.m. as the desert was beginning to settle in for the night, they saw that he had left his watch and bankbook lying on a shelf. A chill of foreboding enveloped them. At that same moment, a massive explosion rattled the earth. Instinctively, they turned toward Francis Mountain and saw the familiar sight of his American flag flying as usual. The next day the sheriff went to investigate. He found one of Earl's boots on the ground beside the mining shaft. There was no other sign of him except some bits of his clothing clinging to a nearby cactus. The house, only a few yards away, was undamaged. On the wall, facing the entry, a freshly painted canvas hung crooked. Earl's last painting was not one of his beloved sunsets. On the canvas he had very carefully painted "LIFE = ?"

In due course, a bulldozer arrived, and now the land is "back to its natural state." There is not so much as a single piece of timber to prove there ever was a house on Francis Mountain. Any evidence to the contrary lies buried in a covered-up mining shaft. Few people make the effort to climb up there. Why should they? There is nothing to see except for that marker, so carefully, yet crudely, hand-tooled by people who remember Earl Francis. Yet, each evening, for one brief moment as the sun is setting, a golden glow touches a stone marker, a weather-beaten boot, and a deserted bird feeder.

It is the only evidence that once there lived a man who carried his house to the top of a mountain.

NOTE: Earl Francis never married or had children. His sister gave me permission in 1971 to use his story and even allowed me to copy parts of his diary, but I have no proof of that and have lost contact with her. Most of the people involved are dead now. It was originally published in a much longer story that included Earl's trip from Washington to Arizona and a (rumored) love triangle that he was involved in. The original story was in one of my earlier books, now out of print.

*Kay Peterson lived full-time in an RV for fifteen years. She traveled in all fifty states and twenty-six other countries. She has written six books on the RV lifestyle. Kay and her husband founded the Escapees RV Club and, in 2001, were inducted into the Motorhome/Recreational Vehicle Hall of Fame in Elkhart, Indiana.*

*Some RVers rate their travels by encounters with bears or beautiful sunsets. Martie rated their trial run by the bathrooms they encountered.*

# Clean Hair

------------------------------

## Martie Mollenhauer

ROUTINES ARE A PART OF OUR LIVES AND JUST BECAUSE WE TOOK the giant courageous leap to seek adventure, we didn't leave the routines home. They just happened in different places

One of my most important routines is morning wash up. Every day I love to wet and lather my hair, massage my scalp and wake up my brain. It is the feeling of clean hair that is so refreshing. I was born with naturally curly or frizzy hair; weather conditions make the difference. It's the humidity of Louisiana or Florida or the dryness of Arizona or New Mexico that take charge. I like to start every day giving my hair a fair chance and then let it do its own thing.

The 21-foot Hi-Lo we took on our trial run came equipped with a tub and shower. We quickly found out that our plastic containers of clothes were best stored there. We would need to use the wash facilities of parks and campgrounds. This was the experience and the challenge. We came to rate our stays by the water temperature and heat in the building, not to mention the water pressure.

In my quest for clean hair, I soon learned I had to be flexible. After a particularly fitful sleep at a campground in Louisiana, we loaded up our little turquoise shower buckets with all of the necessities and went for our walk to the restrooms. There was no heat and the water was lukewarm and that is stretching a point. I was brave enough and forged ahead with a shower because I HAD TO HAVE CLEAN HAIR. Back in the trailer, Bill laughed and called me a liar. Said no way could I have taken a shower. I did! I had to. He didn't get it. For him, it had to be comfort with a capital C, which meant warmth—for me, clean hair.

Some name brand campgrounds often had individual cubicles that were like the lap of luxury. We looked for the signs with the yellow wigwams and weren't disappointed. In fact, we bought a discount card. Only once, when the rodeo came to San Antonio and we stayed near the fairgrounds, did we have to even wait for the showers. No problem though because the greatest conversations were struck up with fellow travelers from all over the world. We were all connected by common threads — our hair.

Once, we pulled into a campground, checked the bathrooms, and drove right out. There was no one in the office and it looked like no one to care for the place either. That night we slept in a motel. I missed the familiarity of the Hi-Lo. After two months it wasn't getting to be like home, it was home.

Our favorite place was at Will Roger's ranch in Claremont, Oklahoma. Imagine Bill's thrill when he talked to the caretaker and found there was a bunkhouse for campers to use complete with private shower and an electric heater. A piece of heaven right in Oklahoma — clean hair and warmth besides.

Sometimes, the walk to the bathrooms was the challenge. We sloshed through the mud, slipped on the ice in Amarillo, and walked through pouring rain. What difference did it make because we had just showered anyhow or were on our way to get wet?

The ones we never quite got used to were the ones where we had to put in the quarters for the water to start and then make sure to have more change so we did not run out mid-washing. And then there was the time when I got all undressed and ready for the shower, put the money in and the water did not come out. It was broken. That was close to a no hair wash day—close.

Sounds like we are obsessive-compulsive, huh? The Hi-Lo is retired before we are, and now we're looking for a fifth wheel for the next journey. We will have the shower right where we are planted; it will be warm and I'll be able to wash my hair everyday.

When we got back home, I found that it took time to let my turquoise shower bucket go. The routines changed, but they never went away. Some things are just a part of who we are.

*Martie Mollenhauer is an early childhood educator and consultant. She and Bill, married thirty-plus years, work and play in New Jersey. She loves reading, writing, quilting, traveling, and people. Their son lives in Australia. Every day in every way she reaches out and makes connections with those in her world. Martie also contributed "The Cocoon."*

# A Cup of Tea
# and Nothing

------------------------------------

## Megan Edwards

FROM SANTA CRUZ, WE HEADED NORTH THROUGH SAN FRANCISCO
and then west out to the Point Reyes Peninsula. Easterners think California has no seasons, but an unmistakable spring was emerging around us,
complete with baby birds and tender green grass.

We stopped at a private campground near the coast. It enjoyed a
delightful location along a stream and was obviously a destination of choice
for families on summer vacation. This time of year, however, the grounds
were populated by permanent residents and overnight visitors like us.

A man and woman were inside the office. The man said, "What is
that thing?" and pointed through the window at the Phoenix, our custom-built, four-wheel-drive office and motorhome. "I've never seen anything like it, and I thought I'd seen them all."

Mark explained and, after we'd signed up for a camping space, asked
if they'd like to see inside. "Sure," they answered in unison, and we trooped
out to the parking lot.

"What kind of engine does she have?" the man asked Mark, and the
two disappeared under the hood. I invited the woman inside.

"Wow," she said. "Wow. This is my dream. I live here in a trailer, but it doesn't move. I dream of the day I can travel." Her eyes took in everything. "Wow," she said again. "You're really doing it." I showed her the back room, the office. She ran her hand over the desk. "Wow. What a perfect place to write. I'm a writer. I always notice desks."

She fell silent as her eyes traveled from floor to ceiling. She seemed to be memorizing every detail. "Wow," she whispered. "Wow."

Suddenly she gave herself a little shake and said, "Gosh, I'm sorry. I really got lost in my thoughts. Thank you for inviting me in. When you're all set up, why don't you come over to my trailer? We can have a cup of tea." Before I could reply, she added, "I'll come knock on your door in an hour or so." She stretched out her hand. "My name's Cherie, by the way."

True to her word, Cherie arrived at the Phoenix an hour later. We walked across the grass toward a row of trailers. Some were huge and new, some were tiny and old. Cherie's was a little one surrounded by red geraniums and two large propane tanks. It looked as though it hadn't rolled in at least a decade.

Inside was a cozy nest just big enough for one. A cat was curled in an armchair, and every nook was filled with a book or a potted plant. A tiny desk stood near the door, and the teakettle was beginning to whistle on the two-burner stove.

"Do you like almond tea?" Cherie asked.

"My favorite," I said.

"I've written a book," said Cherie as she moved the cat and invited me to sit down. "Would you like to see it?"

"Sure," I said, and she opened a box under the desk. She handed me a small volume with a pen-and-ink drawing on the cover. The title was "Nothing."

"Nothing?" I said aloud.

"Nothing," said Cherie, and she laughed. "Yep, it's a book about nothing."

And it was indeed a book about nothing. As we drank our tea, Cherie explained how she'd gotten to a point in her life where she'd lost Everything, which meant, of course, that she had Nothing. "I suddenly realized that Nothing was Something in its own right," she said, "And I started working on the book."

I turned the pages, and the drawings were as important as the words. I sat there, let my tea get cold, and read the whole thing.

"Wow," I said at last. "Wow." It was wonderful.

Cherie and I sat in her little trailer until the sun went down. Two days later, when we left, she said, "Happy Trails!" I never got her last name. I've never seen *Nothing* in a bookstore.

I like to think that Cherie is on the road somewhere, living her dream. Wherever she is, I'm glad our paths crossed that April afternoon. I'm especially grateful for what she gave me, a cup of tea and Nothing.

*When a wildfire destroyed her home in the hills above Los Angeles, Megan Edwards seized the opportunity that her sudden "stufflessness" offered. She hit the road with her husband and dog in their custom-built Phoenix One. "A Cup of Tea and Nothing" is excerpted from her book* Roads From the Ashes: An Odyssey in Real Life on the Virtual Frontier. *The adventure continues on-line at www.RoadTripAmerica.com.*

*New experiences delight the RVer. Thanks to a free coupon and muggy hot weather, Joei was thoroughly delighted with her new experience.*

# Fine Bit of Madness

Joei Carlton Hossack

NEARING THE END OF THE FILM *ZORBA THE GREEK*, ZORBA dances by himself. His arms are spread out and his hands are open toward heaven. He shouts, "Everybody needs a little madness." Well that's my story and I'm sticking to it.

I had just spent five days camping at a Good Sam Rally in Centreville, Michigan. Although the staff members were most welcoming, the participants warm and friendly, and there were plenty of activities and lots of entertainment, the rally seemed endless. The temperature soared to over 95 degrees every day with a humidity index that pushed the temperature to above 105 before noon. To add to our misery, we were not permitted to use our air conditioners because of insufficient power at the fairgrounds. My camper became a mini-sauna. If horses sweat and men perspire and women glow—then I became a Christmas tree in July.

It was our last morning. I had my coffee and said my good-byes to a few new acquaintances. I was waiting in a slow-moving line at one of the two dumping stations. During my hour-long wait I perused the plastic box sitting on the hump in the center of my truck containing my CDs, maps, a couple of dollar-off coupons at various campgrounds, and lo and behold, a one-day pass to a nudist colony in Michigan. It had been sitting, gathering dust, for over a year.

Michigan is a big state. I decided to check it out on the map, just to kill some time. Union City, by all my calculations, looked about fifty miles away and in the direction that I was heading. I had one extra day until I had to be at my next appointment. Before modesty could take hold, my brain went into overdrive and all I could think about was diving into a cool swimming pool—naked.

Madness, I tell you. It was sheer madness. I have never done anything like this, nor have I really seriously contemplated doing anything like this. I called the campground and discovered that the pass was still good and "Yes, I could camp there overnight." The drive was on back roads and since I suspected that they did NOT have billboards advertising their whereabouts, I called when I reached Union City and got specific directions. I was amazed at my calmness. I still believe that my moistness was due to the weather and not anxiety.

Not knowing what to expect, and knowing full well that I wouldn't run into anyone with whom I was even slightly acquainted, I felt I would probably go (largely) unnoticed as most over-fifty, gray-haired, bespectacled, (pleasingly) plump women do. After arriving and checking in I was given (fully-clothed by a fully-clothed guide) a tour of the facilities. The volleyball court, indoor swimming pool and hot tub, lake with boats for rowing and fishing, a sandy beach, and outdoor conversation pool were first rate and inviting in my book.

For my first venture or should I say "adventure" I decided on the conversation pool.

(A) The first thing that struck me funny was that when I went to strip off my clothes in my camper I was tempted to close the blinds.

(B) Everyone who passed me on the path greeted me and smiled. They gave me the once-over like I was still twenty years old. This was done with a look and a smile. There was no ogling or leering or smirking. I, of course, did the same.

(C)  In the conversation pool I was immediately acknowledged and made comfortable enough to join into the conversation. I confessed that this was my first nudist experience and I was admired for my bravery.

From the conversation pool a group, myself included, went to the mud bath.

Another first experience. Chivalry prevailed. A hand was extended so that I wouldn't slip. Conversation flowed as it had done in the pool. We scrubbed and rinsed off in the lake and unfamiliar hands gently washed the mud from my back.

That afternoon in front of the wide-screen television set in the lounge I was approached by familiar faces.

"Hi," the couple said, "had we known that you were a nudist we would have spoken to you about it at the camping rally this morning.

"This morning," I responded, "I wasn't a nudist." (So much for not running into anyone I know.)

That evening I danced, totally uninhibited, to music on the new jukebox with friends I had met in the pool.

The experience, on a scale of one to ten, was easily a twelve. I am still an over-fifty, bespectacled, gray-haired, (pleasingly) plump woman who mostly goes unnoticed in a crowd. Thanks to the one day at Turtle Lake in Union City, Michigan, I'm back to feeling the way I should—feminine, beautiful, and desirable. The toughest thing about my one-day of madness occurred the next morning when I had to put my clothes back on and go out into the big, anonymous world.

Would I do it again?  In a minute—as soon as the sunburn stops stinging.


*Joei Carlton Hossack, a full-time, solo RVer, is the author of* Everyone's Dream Everyone's Nightmare; Kiss This Florida, I'm Outta Here; A Million Miles From Home; Alaska Bound and Gagged; Free Spirit, Born to Wander; *and* Chasing The Lost Dream. *All six books are available through Amazon.com or http://www.JoeiCarlton.com. She is a columnist for the* Gypsy Journal. *Joei also contributed "Agony of De-Feet."*

# Animal Crossing

REMEMBER, RHINOCEROSES *ALWAYS* HAVE THE RIGHT-OF-WAY
BY DONNA SAUTER

On one of my trips I drove through the Wildlife Safari near Roseburg, Oregon. While in the lion compound, a shaggy old fellow decided he wanted my share of the road. The lion ran alongside my Coachman Class C motorhome. My heart pounded, my hands were frozen on the wheel. Then suddenly he crossed in front of us and ambled off into the field. And, just before the lion, I had spotted a huge rhinoceros grazing on the hillside above the road. For a moment I panicked. At the gate they'd told us, "Remember, the rhino always has the right-of-way." Oh, yes indeed, I'd let any of them have any part of the road they wanted.

## SAM THE CAT BY CAROLYN TALBOT

Sam, our fifteen-year-old cat, loved to explore our various campsites on our journeys. As we prepared to leave Red Lodge, Montana, I assumed my husband had rounded up Sam and put him in the camper. Of course, he thought I had. Sure enough, when I put out the supper dishes in Cody, Wyoming, that night, Sam was nowhere to be found. We called the campground and left a frantic message. I couldn't just sit and wait, so I gathered a kitty overnight bag, some things for me, and took off back to Red Lodge. It was dusk when I arrived. The lady in charge said they had found Sam in the trees around our site, wondering where his house had gone. After giving me a big piece of his mind, Sam came to me. We spent the night in Red Lodge and rejoined the family next morning.

The second time we left Sam behind was . . . .

*In preparing for her trip to Nahanni Valley in the Northwest Territories, Michele did not plan for an encounter with a bear.*

# Bear Escapade

Michele Lorenz

I HAD JUST LEFT THE DENÉ NATIVE ARTS CENTER AND WAS PLEASED with my purchase of a traditional birch bark basket with porcupine quill decoration. It had been steadily raining all day, and the road I was traveling on east toward Fort Simpson was slick with sticky mud and only tundra-type terrain as far as the eye could see. Two-foot high ridges of mud ran along both sides of the road, where wet mud is regularly scraped to maintain travel, much like we might see during a winter snowstorm. It seemed odd, but so did many experiences in this fascinating Northwest Territory.

Fort Simpson was my connection point to a fly-in day trip I had planned to the Nahanni Valley, up the Mackenzie River. This famous valley had intrigued me since reading about a couple who had lived there in the '50s, their experiences chronicled in many stories of the region. Unfortunately it is accessible only by boat via the MacKenzie River, and, for the short-on-time vacationer, only a fly-over with stops gives one a sense of it. I was excited about this long-awaited adventure.

I headed to the only campground in Fort Simpson proper, driving my second rig, "Emily," a late '60s Dodge mini-motorhome, which basically was a glorified 20-foot camper van. Emily was coated with gray-beige mud, along with my bike that had been strapped to the rear spare tire. The bicycle was a gift from a friend and I had only protected the seat, gears, and handle grips with flimsy plastic bags that were beginning to shred.

As I pulled into the campground, situated in a low shallow area near the river with lots of foliage, I noticed there were none of the "bear proof" garbage cans seen throughout British Columbia and the Yukon. At check-in the managers indicated that, yes, indeed there were bear visitations to the campground "for the garbage," but that if one kept a clean camp you would be okay. I noticed there were some tent campers, several open sites, and many overflowing garbage cans. I surveyed the sites and selected one that had the least bush surrounding it and was farthest from the garbage.

I was nervous, but had no other choice—there was no handy Wal-Mart or the like to pull into. It was late in the day and I was concentrating on what was needed to make tomorrow's visit to Nahanni. I had my dinner, careful to dispose of all remnants of food in the open garbage bins. As I returned to my rig, I looked around the bush for any signs of the black furries munching. I again noticed my bicycle with thickly caked mud all over, but there was no time or water source to wash. As I dozed off, I thought my friend would be aghast that I had allowed this to happen.

Around 3 a.m. I was aroused from my sleep by a grunting and rubbing sound near my bedside window. I rolled over, but it did not abate. I then slid open the curtains to see a big shadow and no bike. As my eyes focused, I saw a bear steadily licking at my bike seat and handle grips. I pounded on the window yelling "No, no!" but he remained, apparently enthralled with the scents and salt of my seat and handles. I threw off my covers, stood up and realized all my bear education did not prepare me for what to do when inside your camper!

I say I stood up, but in this model camper there was only one area to do so, which was the dropped floor, about twelve inches wide by eight feet long. I paced a few times in this space trying to decide what to do. Before my brain could compute, the floor beneath me suddenly rose, and to my horror I realized the bear was now underneath the van! My mind started reeling. I knew the deterioration of the materials underneath me, of the rusted undercoating, now almost thirty years old. Would it hold? Would he come through for me? Where was my flashlight?

It appeared that he might have located the gray water tank, and, of course, there were probably odors—oh, why didn't I dump? Oh yes, there was no dump remember? His sounds had now advanced to snorting and whooshing. The van was visibly moving side to side as if on a stormy sea. My God would he, could he, overturn this thing with me in it?

Juvenile behavior overtook me and I began a stomping tantrum yelling, "Get out!" This had no effect whatsoever. Somewhere in the back of my mind, I remembered a motto from a safety-conscious RVing Women seminar: "Worse case scenario, when you have a motorhome, you can start up your engine and leave."

I scampered for my keys—hearing growls along with the drooling and snorting—launched into the driver's seat, and started the engine. Almost instantly, the van returned to even keel and the bear went for the bush!

After heart palpitations diminished and I collected my senses, I spent the remainder of the early dawn hours lying down with keys and flashlight in hand, unable to return to sleep. I recall arriving at the airfield a little after 6 a.m. for my 10 a.m. flight, and, yes, despite only one day in the Nahanni, it was worth it all, even with the bear escapade.

*Michele Lorenz has been a working solo full-timer for three years, and is well-traveled throughout the American and Canadian West. She describes herself as a gypsy at heart who believes in living life with courage and balance. Favorite Campsite: Alpine Lake in the Cascades where I can kayak, hike, make baskets, meditate on nature's wonders, and watch my cats frolic with the local critters. Favorite Bumper Sticker: "Real Women Drive Dodge Diesels."*

# *Exit Ramp*

## THE THING ABOUT TRAVELING WITH PETS IS . . .

✍ their size. *MC*

✍ I don't. I have enough trouble looking after myself. *BC*

✍ dogs in general (and Dusty in particular) have such enthusiasm for their new surroundings that is contagious. *DW*

✍ their joy in finding new sights and smells everywhere we go —that is, after the look of shock wears off when we open the door and the world has changed. *MS*

✍ I'm too lazy and do not have a pet. *NA*

✍ how so many people are pet lovers and stop to pet my dog, giving me a chance to meet someone new. *SB*

✍ I love cats. I am thrilled when I meet someone who is traveling with a cat or two. I ask outright if I can visit so I can have my kitty-fix. *CT*

✍ our cat was adopted by the people who bought our house and had three cats. As difficult as it was in the beginning, having the cat with us would have added to the stress. *LE*

✍ I traveled years with a small dog. As much as I love animals, at this time in my life, now that I am older, without is better. *DS*

✍ I don't. I have two (stuffed) bears who are very good travelers. *DE*

✍ they keep you on your toes and look silly in the driver's seat. *CC*

# Relationships

-----------------------------------

*Imagine living in 250 square feet or less, 24 hours a day, 7 days a week. This presents special challenges, sometimes insurmountable, as our writers share.*

*According to a survey on the RV lifestyle, Nicky discovered that RVers NEVER fight. Hmmmmm.*

# The Survey

Nicky Boston

WE RECENTLY PARTICIPATED IN A SURVEY THAT ASKED ABOUT A hundred questions regarding the RV lifestyle. The survey covered everything from the adjustments between a stick house and steadfast community to the ebb and flow of wheeled living and the lack of a constant environment. The study's conclusions put us among the highest in intelligence and likened us to the spirit of pioneers. The results made us feel very special as we almost fit right in.

The one issue that surprised us was that, according to the survey, RVers don't fight! We don't argue with our mates nor seem possessed of any negative thoughts, irritating habits, or short tempers. Hmmm. Are we the only ones who would admit that perhaps a voice might be raised while, for instance, helping the other partner back into an empty campground space? Might there be some little disagreement concerning one partner's choice of objects deemed unnecessary by the other partner such as that THIRD pair of tennis shoes (oh so comfortable) or that DISREPUTABLE OLD FADED T-SHIRT (also oh so comfortable and a favorite)?

Talking to our friends who compiled the survey, we discovered we were one of only three couples who admitted to a slight flare-up or two.

However, we'll keep going and try to perfect this uncommon trait for about, at least, ten years. If we still haven't achieved the "norm," then we'll practice for a few more years.

If you hear slightly raised voices when approaching our rig, just give us a few minutes. It's only a small lapse and should fade away as we remember that RVers *never* fight.


*Nicky Boston also contributed "Addiction" and "September 11."*

*Communication, ever a challenge between travel partners, becomes
more so when backing up the RV. Susan relates a particularly
trying incident with a new rig on a rainy night
on the Blue Ridge Parkway.*

# Backing Up

Susan Campbell

AH, THE INTENSE JOY OF THE HIGHEST LEVEL OF COMMUNICATION
between couples: the ecstasy of movement that a couple can share, the
mutual fulfillment of timing, the little intimate special language of a couple,
the correct speed of movement, and a successful entry.

Yes, I mean backing your RV into the campsite.

All couples must come to grips with backing up, and couples must
communicate to perform the task. Therein lies the problem. My husband
backs up like a Martian while I'm giving him Venus directions. Oh, we
have been a pas de deux of grace and precision, sometimes even getting
applause and verbal accolades from our camping neighbors. We were doing
great until a new rig entered our life.

I had always wondered about the women who never get out of the rig
to direct the backing up or the occasional woman standing there, refusing
to give directions even when a crunching sound is the only clue to the
driver. Avoidance is now part of my pattern, sort of like getting a headache.
Several times I have volunteered to go for groceries while he got the rig
parked, or I made moving day the same day I was scheduled to work.

Truths I have learned about backing up:

- After dark there will be no level campsites.
- Your husband's hearing will decline.
- If you use walkie talkies, your camping neighbors can hear you and may even offer suggestions.
- If you use walkie talkies, the batteries will run out at crucial moments.
- When the campground owner wants to park you, it will always be an easy parking job in a level space, usually a pull-through.
- The best parking tip ever is to hit the side of the rig with your hand to stop the driver. Of course, this only works with a motorhome.
- If you enjoy nature, you'll often find back-in spaces from hell. They will be around the curve, just missing the big tree where your RV must show the flexibility of a Yoga instructor.
- In competition with a rearview camera, the man will prefer the electronic device to his wife.

Am I too sensitive about not being noticed? Is it wrong to want attention from my husband? Here is the way I see it. The person giving the directions should be the authority figure. The driver should follow the hand movements of the person who can actually see the rig and its entry into the space, the ground, the surrounding trees, the hookups. Our current problems stem from my competition with the backup camera, and frankly, I'm losing. I have considered flashing to get his attention but my ego could be damaged—that television screen is irresistible.

The lowest point in our parking history came shortly after we bought a new motorhome. We were traveling the Blue Ridge Parkway, which is a wonderful drive, but challenging with its narrow, curving roads. It was raining off and on for several days, always raining when we were ready to find our campsite for the night. Each campground was proving to be a challenge in finding a space where we could level the rig, so we would have to try several spaces. Each time I would get out with the umbrella, trying to be a good sport about the adverse conditions. The third night we were having a particularly hard time—especially my husband who was not following my hand signals. Maybe he was having trouble seeing me in the pouring rain. I came to the driver's side to talk to him, to calmly explain my hand signals. He couldn't hear me because the window was closed. I asked him to open it and he told me he couldn't—he would get wet. Yep, he actually said, "I can't, I'm getting wet" to the person standing out in the rain. Did I mention it was pouring rain?

It was one of the pivotal moments in a marriage. My husband swears to this day that he was concerned about the inside of the rig getting wet. I have forgiven, but not forgotten.

*Susan Campbell has traveled extensively all her adult life. Mid-life crisis led to having a baby when she was forty and the idea of traveling in an RV (to carry baby stuff around). What was to be a several-year trip has evolved into fourteen years of full-time RV travel. Daughter Samantha's story appears on page 56.*

# Yield Right-of-Way

*Since we, your editors, know that some RVers DO fight, here are two tips to help diffuse disagreements.*

### THE SATURDAY SOLUTION BY ALICE ZYETZ

To reduce the fussing with your partner, save the discussions about what irritates you until Saturday, AND you are not allowed to write down the issues. Considering the growing incidence of short-term memory loss, the Saturday technique reduces most of the arguments because you usually can't remember what bothered you the previous Tuesday. If you still do remember it, then the tremendous emotion is gone but you can discuss what the real hurt was and then do the listening and negotiation to resolve it.

### ARGUMENTS BY THE NUMBER BY NANCY VINESKI—
### AS LEARNED FROM DEANNA WHITE,
### WHO LEARNED IT FROM LISA JACKSON

Whenever you're having a disagreement about something like where to park, what to do, where to eat, communicate on a scale of one to ten how important it is to you, with ten being the most important. Sometimes we'll be arguing about where to go for lunch and it doesn't matter to me but Tom will say, "It's an eight to me; I really want Mexican food." For me maybe I'm about a two and a half, so it solves the problem. Most of the time it works out that way. If it's much more important to one of you than the other, that makes the decision. Once in a while it does happen that you're both up there at an eight or nine. Then you'll probably fight it out until you identify what it is and work out a solution.

*The five most essential words for a healthy and vital relationship are "I apologize" and "You are right."*

*For some, living with a partner twenty-four hours a day, seven*
*days a week, can throw the relationship into a tailspin.*
*Most people don't discuss that aspect of RVing.*
*Lainie shares her story.*

# Living Together 24/7

- - - - - - - - - - - - - - - - - - - - - - - - - - - - - -

### Lainie Epstein

MY HUSBAND JERRY AND I DOVE HEAD FIRST INTO FULL-TIMING
in June 2001. We did a fair amount of research ahead of time, as much as
one can do while selling a house, working full-time, and preparing for the
unknown. We checked RV discussion forums for recommendations of
various sorts and, of course, had our own vision of what our new life
would be like. I don't recall running across anything regarding how living
together 24/7 would impact our relationship. Well, if I did I wasn't pay-
ing attention. After all, we acknowledged we had a strong relationship
and got along and it wouldn't be an issue.

So you can imagine how stunned I was when only two months later
I found myself sobbing into a pay phone next to a soft drink machine in
front of a busy supermarket on a Sunday afternoon. My good friend,
Patty, listened and gave her professional advice while I confessed that our
marriage was in jeopardy.

Jerry and I had met later in life and were brought together by common interests in bicycling, backpacking, camping, and other activities
that kept us fit and out-of-doors. We bought a house, eventually married,
and by the time we headed out on our new adventure had known each

other for ten years—enough time to have endured multiple changes in our lives that required a degree of adaptability.

We had also developed a basic design of how we problem-solved and interacted, which involved a lot of individual independence. We had jobs in completely different fields with different schedules. I was in health care working days, nights, and weekends, while Jerry was in research and development working weekdays 8 to 5. We had our own interests and friends that kept us busy and happy without each other's company. Our common interests and friends also kept us busy, happy, and playing together. We even took short, separate vacations and during our mutual vacations we got along famously for two weeks at a time.

The initial transition to our new lifestyle was painful. Jerry is my best friend and life partner. What was happening? No longer having the work routine and friends nearby is difficult. We enjoy the same activities but doing them together all the time had become stressful rather than enjoyable as it had once been. What had worked for us before was not working in this situation. This lifestyle was highlighting the weaknesses. Even if we had returned to our former life (which we considered), the problem would remain. The same themes that were there before RV life had raised their ugly heads. And there was no escape.

After a hit-and-run accident, we became single-minded as we had a big problem to deal with: insurance company, repairs to two vehicles, etc. We do well in crisis mode. We also had to rearrange our loose itinerary and ended up at the Escapees Club RV park in Benson, Arizona. The RV was awaiting parts and repairs in Tucson. Settling down for a while allowed us to meet a community of RVers and gave both of us the outlet we needed. It gave us a stable place in which to pursue our own interests. And it gave me an opportunity to get to know other women. I boldly asked a few about how *they* got along with their mates in this lifestyle. Answers varied and didn't quite fit us.

Patty had drawn broad strokes for me on the phone that day in August. Her advice was invaluable. I have gradually been able to adapt it to who we are as individuals and as a couple. Jerry and I will always have disagreements, but we are learning how to deal with them in different ways. Figuring out what works and what doesn't is tricky. Relationships are dynamic and always in need of work, adjustments, and compromise. Each relationship is unique. What works for one is not necessarily appropriate for another relationship. This may be why few talk about it. It is a very personal experience, not like figuring out cell phone service or buying solar panels, which people can and do talk about in great length.

So what happened between the initial crisis and the present? The crisis was pivotal. Our inability to fight constructively was key. I can become emotional and nonverbal, Jerry wants logic and rational discussion. Each of us had to be right and "win" our point of view. The minutiae of life escalated into major arguments. We decided to make rules for our fights. Identifying the issue was important. Are we really having an argument about the misplaced item or is this merely the trigger for an underlying issue? Then we each discuss our view without interruption. Only the issue at hand is to be addressed. Using sentences that begin with "I feel" or "I think" keeps things in perspective. Mostly *really* listening and being respectful is important. We have managed to diffuse the smaller things quickly. The larger issues occur less frequently. There has certainly been some consciousness-raising for the both of us. Who I think I am is not necessarily how my husband sees me.

Are we fixed? Nah! We are a work in progress.


*Lainie Epstein is an avid birder. She loves the surprise of finding birds; enjoying their beauty, behaviors, and song; and the challenge of identification. Her physical activity centers around bicycling, hiking, and running. Indoor interests are reading and handcrafts. Lainie has a long list of things she wants to learn.*

# Hanging up the Keys

---

Llorene Myers

LIVING IN AN RV WAS NOTHING NEW TO MY HUSBAND AND ME. Since we had lived in a 23-foot Winnie in the late '70s for a year, being on the road again in 1989 in a 30-foot fifth wheel was familiar. My husband was a computer contractor. As we traveled for his contracts, I did temporary office work when we settled for any length of time. We both enjoyed the variety of work experiences in the mobile lifestyle.

One of the beauties of living on wheels is the ability to get up and go at will. Several times, a contract would end, we'd pack up and pull out, sometimes choosing a destination and enjoying our travels until the next job came along. Sometimes we planned these treks in advance, worked our last day and left the next morning. How many people today can do that?

Living as a full-timer had its unique share of challenges, but there were some days that were especially challenging. You learn quickly what's most important when you find yourself in below-zero weather in Minnesota, your holding tanks freeze, and you can't use the toilet. You're forced to bring in water in jugs, warm the tanks with portable heaters strategically placed in the underbelly, walk through the snow to use a pit toilet—even during the night—*and* heat water on the stovetop to take a sponge bath. What *fun*!

Life for me was altered dramatically after my divorce and my life on the road ended. I found myself going through changes again — this time, alone. I not only had to deal with the separation issues, but also with many other lifestyle concerns. Believe me, living in zero weather in Minnesota sometimes sounded good.

Coming to terms and dealing with the divorce ended up in my lap because my soon-to-be ex-husband was still on the road. Sitting before a divorce attorney and spilling my guts was both embarrassing and unsettling, not to mention the logistics of finding him to serve papers. Luckily at that point, we were still friends and he gave me an address for the paperwork. It seemed insurmountable to recreate my life history as a single woman after a twenty-year marriage. I didn't think I could do it, but I did. Our divorce was amicable enough at the time and our issues were few, as we had no children—a big issue for most couples. It was a given that the rig would be mine, so I arranged to split our belongings and brought it home. My ex-husband bought his own motorhome and continues to live on the road.

Not only was it a divorce from him, but from his family as well. Divorce has a way of separating you from people who once were a big part of your life. Relations were strained with one family during the separation and communication from the others has been slight, if at all. Maybe someday we will reconnect, but for now, we have little contact.

One of the most difficult things I experienced was losing my connection to the RVers I'd come to know and cherish for nearly ten years. Unfortunately, our paths had diverged. Through all of this, having close ties to my own family was my saving grace. I lived in my rig parked on my sister's property for more than a year and was lucky that we all got along exceptionally well. Fortunately, I was given the opportunity to rent a home from them on property they had recently purchased with a house on it. I moved out of the trailer, got my personal stuff out of storage after ten years, and moved in.

The following year, I sold my old truck and trailer to a man who had lost his house in a fire and needed a place to live. The night he came to pick it up was a tough one. It was a sad sight to see my traveling home leaving me for the last time with a stranger behind the wheel. I know a piece of my heart left with my rig that day.

I began establishing myself and now have a permanent position in an area where I was raised and had called home when I would come to visit family in the past. Even so, I still long for the road. I find myself looking at RVs when I'm driving and wonder where they're going. Is it for a weekend, a vacation, or are they enjoying extended travel and life as I once knew it? If I had a steady source of income, I would return—at least for a few more years. I feel very lucky to have traveled the way I did at such a young age when most of the people I met were much older and most people my age were still in the workaday world. I treasure all the places I've been, the people I've met. When I look at my photo albums, I relive the day the pictures were taken and think how fortunate I was to have had those experiences.

*Llorene Myers is a former Escapees member, who lived for ten years on the road in a fifth wheel, and is now in a house in the state of Washington. She works for a laboratory on the Hanford reservation and keeps in touch with Boomers and other women on the road.*

# Exit Ramp

## MY FAMILY THINKS . . .

✍ we get bored—HA! *MC*

✍ it's cool to be traveling all over the country—well, one daughter does, the other doesn't. *BC*

✍ mail forwarding is a myth and they never send me anything. *MS*

✍ I'll come to my senses sooner or later. *NA*

✍ I'm being irresponsible because I left a good job and don't I miss my grandchildren. *AF*

✍ we have chosen a wonderful lifestyle. They like that we can come for long visits. *SB*

✍ my lifestyle is intriguing, but I don't think they understand how spontaneous and casual we are now. *CT*

✍ we are on vacation all the time, that we are in that frame of mind all the time. *LE*

✍ we are lucky to be able to live our dream. My mom (82 at this writing) answers the question, "Where's Janet?" with "She's home." *JW*

✍ it's neat that Al and I can "live our dream." *DE*

✍ I'm never going to grow up. *CC*

✍ RVing has brought joy to our lives. My daughter and son-in-law plan to go full-time at age 55. *DS*

# Going Your
# Own Way

- - - - - - - - - - - - - - - - - - - - - - - -

*Some women travel alone by choice. In other cases, circumstances—a divorce or death of a spouse—may leave a woman without her travel partner. She may decide to keep traveling on her own. These women share stories of what it is like being a solo traveler.*

*Learning to travel alone for a woman is more than mastering the black tank. Betty recounts the challenges and riches she has found traveling solo.*

# Going It Single

Betty Prange

"HEY LITTLE LADY, YOU SURE LOOK LIKE YOU KNOW HOW TO do that."

I looked up from connecting the sewer hose to my motorhome.

"My wife won't do that. How does your husband get you to do it?"

I straightened up and looked him in the eye. "Ohhh," imitating his good-old-boy demeanor, "he up and died on me."

There are plenty of challenges to being a single, nomadic RV woman, but hooking up a sewer hose isn't one of them. Struggling with the RV dealership that wants to brush off my concerns is a challenge. Toiling with a propane refrigerator, which does not want to stay lit, is a frustration. Discovering that the route mapped out along Oklahoma secondary roads is closed due to flash flooding is downright scary when there is no navigator sitting beside me to check alternatives, and there is no place to stop and check the map myself. Finding the electrical system, which activates my jacks and slide-outs, has shorted out for the twentieth time is an obstacle that brings on rage. Just learning to be single, learning to find joys in being alone, is enough of a challenge after many years in a companionable, adventuresome, and fulfilling marriage.

I am learning to take full responsibility for maintenance, something I felt ill-prepared to do. Friends who are willing to teach me, a warranty on the motorhome, and cash reserves help me get by. I manage. But life isn't all about driving and maintaining my home on wheels. It is still about the things I loved when my husband, Lin, and I traveled together: new places, new experiences, new culinary delights, and new people. Meeting people takes on a new perspective in my single state. People start conversations with one person when they might hesitate for fear of intruding when there are two. John Steinbeck's *Travels with Charley* and William Least Heat Moon's *Blue Highways* are full of stories of people they met while traveling without human companions.

Many people, men and women, express astonishment that I drive a 35-foot motorhome with tow car on my own. "Aren't you scared, don't you carry a gun or have a big dog with you?" The answers are "No." Guns scare me more than the thought of someone trying to harm me. I decided a long time ago that good sense and confidence are better protection than force.

I may think other people's amazement is unfounded. Yet I expressed a similar sentiment the day my motorhome broke down in Nevada, 101 miles from the nearest repair facility. While I waited for the tow truck, a woman pulled up on a motorcycle with Yukon plates. Intrigued, I struck up a conversation. This 70ish-year-old woman was riding her bike, camping along the way, from the Arctic Circle to southern Mexico. She would meet up with other bikers in Mexico, but was making most of the trip solo. I was impressed and told her so. I heard in my voice the incredulousness people express toward me. So why shouldn't she be riding a motorcycle to Mexico? To me it seemed daring only because it was outside my realm of experience. I vowed not to act amazed at future encounters, only to ask questions and learn about others' lifestyles. Who knows, maybe someday I will want to ride a motorcycle from one end of the continent to the other.

Once timid, I now seek out new experiences and new people; soaring in a glider, riding in ultra lights, soaking in hot springs from Washington to New Mexico, volunteering and working in state parks and a hot spring resort. A month in China convinced me I want to return for an extended stay as an English teacher. On the drawing board is a trip along the Alaskan Marine Highway carrying only a backpack. Fascinating people who share their differing values and lifestyles fill my days. All the time I am reminded of Lin who banished worries and "what-ifs," taking risks to find joy in living instead of retreating to the security of a rocking chair. I too will be adventuresome.

Some singles tell me they feel excluded in an RV world largely populated by couples. That is not true for me. My friends are a rich mix representing all hues of the spectrum in terms of relationships and lifestyles. And when I start feeling sorry for myself because I am alone, I remember the wise words of a single friend. He told me one of the advantages of traveling alone is that there is no one in the passenger seat to point out that you made a wrong turn, scraped a low-hanging branch, or hit a curb pulling into a gas station.

I celebrate new experiences, am proud of the things learned, and hope that by sharing my stories that other women will take the wheel. Women can stay on the road if they lose their partner. Single women can get started on their own. Sometimes it seems overwhelming and I turn to friends for help or even a shoulder to cry on. But more often I laugh with them. I appreciate the friends who stand ready to give me tips when I get stymied, but let me try to make repairs myself. I appreciate, too, the ones who offer swaps so we can both share our skills.

Yes, there are challenges. There are always challenges in life. So, I am changing and rejoicing. But dumping the black water tank? Come on, give me a break. Since women still change the lion's share of diapers in this society, it doesn't seem to me that dumping tanks is much of a challenge.

*Betty has been a full-time RVer since 1993. When her husband, Lin Strout, died of cancer in 1999, she chose to remain a nomad, a lifestyle that suits her. But the most important reason for staying on the road was the community of friends she found there. Betty also contributed "A Day of the Heart."*

*Though she travels with no human companions, Carol, who works on the road, has plenty of company as she travels with two horses, a guard dog, and a cat.*

# Gypsy's Journeys

## Carol Dennis

MY ADVENTURE BEGAN IN 1999 WHEN I PURCHASED MY FIRST HORSE, Lady. She is a Tennessee Walking Horse, dark bay (reddish-brown) with white patches. She reminds me of an Indian pony. I became an avid trail rider and loved to travel and ride around Florida. I bought my second horse, a beautiful young black and white Spotted Saddle Horse whom I named Spirit, so that I could have a spare horse. Riding became a passion.

I found myself traveling more and more with both of my horses, leaving my business in the hands of my manager. I learned a lot of "horse sense" while traveling around Florida, hauling food, water, and other things the horses need. I started dreaming about what it would be like to ride trails in other states.

While out on a trail one day, the thought occurred to me, "Why not just get out of the regular rat race, go on the road, and travel to those other places?" I started thinking about how I could do this and have enough money to pay the bills. The "workamper" concept (RV travelers who work) seemed the most ideal for my situation.

I have always been a person who can jump into any new situation and figure out a way to go about doing it. I put my house on the market, sold my business to my manager, and bought a truck camper so I'd still be able to haul my horse trailer. The slide-out room in the camper makes more room for my cat, guard dog, and me. This way I have my family of pets with me so I never feel lonely or alone.

Where would I travel to first? The magazine *Workamper News* provided an answer. Answering an ad, I contacted a church youth camp in the Hill Country of Texas that had three hundred acres. That would be enough room for my horses and me. The camp director was willing to give it a try. It worked out great and the job was fantastic. I worked outdoors most of the time doing new construction of cabins, mowing fields, painting, taking care of the pool, and many other small jobs. I also learned electrical wiring and some plumbing. I loved the job and meeting new people who also worked on the road.

While there, I rode in some of Texas' state parks. The area in Bandera, Texas, is breathtaking and feels remote. It has mountains and steep challenging trails. My horses were in very fine shape by the time they climbed all the steep hills. They had been used to the flatlands of Florida.

Originally I thought that being on the road and not having many responsibilities would be easy. It's not! Before I began my journeys, I made sure my 1999 Dodge Dually diesel truck was in top condition. However, when I first started out, my truck motor died and I had to spend three extra weeks in north Florida while the motor was rebuilt. It did not seem to matter how well I had kept it up; I was stranded. Thank God I was near my girlfriend's home, and my animals and I were able to stay with her during the repairs.

My next breakdown occurred the very next year when leaving Florida. I hit an object in the highway that caused the fan to come off the motor and damage the radiator and more. Again I was stranded, but a guardian angel appeared in the form of a complete stranger, Jerry. He stopped to ask if I needed help and invited me and my "family" to stay at his home for the next week while I waited for my truck to be repaired. This has always been my saving grace. Always think positive and ask for help and help has always arrived in some form. Jerry and I have become close friends as a result and always will be.

I have been fortunate in all other areas. No other bad things have happened and I am glad for that. The good things have been meeting many new friends along the way and seeing beautiful country, both driving and riding the trails in different states.

I recently decided I needed a home base, some place to go to in the winter. I purchased an eight-acre property in north Florida. As I write this, I am again on the road, stopped for eight weeks in Missouri before heading to South Dakota. I grew up in the suburbs of Kansas City, Missouri, and my sons and grandsons live there now. I am visiting them before my next job in South Dakota.

For a place to stay in Missouri, I located a beautiful bed and breakfast near them by looking in the U.S. Stable Guide. Western Way Bed and Breakfast is owned by Bill and Connie Green. After I explained how I work on the road in exchange for a place to hook up, they contacted me, deciding to give me a try. Connie and Bill live in an attractive log home on fifty-five acres with a log guest house beside it. On the property is a covered arena with horse stalls inside.

As a kid I had always pictured and dreamed of riding my own horse across the open fields and hills. When I lived here as a city girl, there was no way to keep a horse. Now I'll have eight weeks to ride my home state and see it from another perspective.

From here I will head north to spend three months in Keystone, South Dakota. I found listings on the Internet under guest ranches of North America and will be helping out at a working ranch up near the Black Hills and Custer State Park.

I have always believed "If you can dream it, you can do it." If there is something that you want, take hold of your dreams and just go do it because life does not wait for you. You must make it happen!

*Carol Dennis, the Gypsy Groomer, is a single lady, age fifty-four, traveling with two horses, her cat, and her dog.*

# Side Roads

## BORDER CROSSING BY LINDA WILLARD

I approached Canadian Customs at White Rock, British Columbia, my cat's papers and mine in order. My RV was neat and clean and the curtains were open. The sign in front of me said, "Speed bumps— slow to 25." Miles an hour or kilometers? I wasn't sure.

I think it was miles, but even as I slowed I'll never forget those three huge bumps. As I reached the first one, I already knew it was too late. All hell broke loose behind me. The three house plants flew off the table. Wet potting soil was everywhere. The TV toppled off the shelf and dangled midair. All the drawers in the cupboards opened and dumped their contents. The two water jugs spilled. If it was possible to slide, fall, or sail through the air, it did, mixing soil, water and cat litter.

Up in the dish cupboard all was quiet, but the smell of kerosene permeated the air. I'd put the lamp there to keep the cat from knocking it over. Now its contents lay coating all the dishes on the shelves. With this mess I approached Canadian Customs. A pleasant lady asked the usual questions, the first one being, "Do you have a license plate on this THING?" (In North Carolina we have plates only on the rear.) She looked through the window but didn't comment.

Her next question was, "Why are you traveling alone?" And her third: "Are you carrying anything to protect yourself?" A very loaded question.

I know that it is not legal to carry pepper spray into Canada, but I would tell the truth. No use lying and then having it found on me during a search. So I told her I did carry spray with me when traveling alone.

"Where is it?" she asked.

"In my handbag."

She paused a minute, then said, "Just keep it in there and get out of here." And I did. Welcome to Canada!

*After suddenly losing her husband, Barbara decided to*
*continue RVing and slowly gained confidence*
*in her ability to manage alone.*

# Alone

Barbara Cormack

I WOKE UP FIVE YEARS AGO AND MY LIFE WAS GONE. MY husband went to work one day and didn't come home. He was killed in a car accident. My two daughters were in the car too, badly injured. After spending a year getting them back on their feet, I was able to look at my life, including the 35-foot Bounder sitting in my driveway. Do I sell it? That was not an option; I owed too much on it. Do I keep it? I really couldn't afford to run it, but our lifestyle had revolved around RVing so I decided to jump in by myself.

After procrastinating for weeks with my stomach in knots, one day I kicked myself in the butt and got in the Bounder. First thing I did was go to a BIG parking lot with no cars, set up barriers, and learn to back up this monster. During that first year I watched the white line going down the highway and then decided that I should watch where I was going instead. Finally my instinct kicked in. First trip was a two-hour drive to the stock car races. Panic set in about a week before I was leaving. I worried myself sick, couldn't eat, couldn't sleep, wondering how I was going to get gas, what if the generator wouldn't work. Well I did make it after running the batteries dead and having a flat tire. Thank goodness for

Emergency Road Assistance. Every year I branched out further and did more difficult things: tollgates, border crossings, small towns with narrow roads, very narrow bridges, the state of Florida, and dealing with barriers in construction sites.

After taking friends along for help for three years, I knew it was time to go on long trips by myself. As a woman, I had learned I needed to make things as easy as possible, and everything had to be lightweight since I had no arm strength. I purchased a tow hitch that weighed only seventeen pounds and a WIDE squeegee to clean my motorhome, saving a lot of wear and tear on the old body when using it. I had to remember to not let anyone intimidate me whether it has to do with repairs, filling up with gas, or having a hothead behind me just itching to pass. I also never let someone else direct me into a camping spot; I do it myself. I learned to stay in the middle lane in big cities, ignoring the truckers going by.

My first long trip, lasting two months, was to the east coast of Canada where I was born. I took all the thruways, as there were lots of service centers and rest areas. I did a lot of going around in circles since they don't make many service stations to accommodate our big rigs. I learned how to read maps very fast. I now have a written page beside me with every exit I need. I replaced ten-hour driving days with about five hours a day, sometimes less. I stayed at one campground in Halifax for the summer and did all my exploring in my car. I did come back down the next year and explored a lot more in my motorhome. Boy I am getting good. I went to Florida last winter for three months, back along the east coast of Canada this summer.

Dumping my tanks is a breeze, but I don't get too sure of myself. Dumping my black is always first, then the gray. One time I had forgotten to close my gray water and thankfully realized it before my hose got too full in the compartment. I double-check my car to make sure it's in neutral, the parking brake off, and the car locked. I have heard what happens when you don't: burned out motor or transmission. I remember to take the key out every night or I will have a dead battery. The water pump must be off and all liquid containers securely put away. When I get on the highway and hear an unexpected noise, I start to cry from frustration because I can't stop and find out what it is. Later I discover a couple of full drawers have fallen, or the refrigerator has opened on its own and a jar has broken and pickles are rolling all over the floor. I swear, I scream, I throw myself on the bed and cry at this person who has made my life hell because of the accident. Getting this out of my system, I carry on.

I have now graduated to living in my motorhome most of the year, but still can't give up the house and the stuff. Canadians can only be out of the country six months of the year. At the moment I am working my way back home, having been on the road as far as Palm Springs, California. The one thing that is very hard for me is accomplishing something for the first time and having no one to tell it to. Am I lonely? Yes, but if I waited for someone to go with me, I would never leave home. My stomach doesn't act up any more, but I still worry a little about getting stuck in a situation that I won't be able to get out of.

I love the opportunities to meet interesting people, like a fellow who ran the Iditerod in Alaska and a reporter from England. I am learning about the country and how beautiful it is, both in Canada and the United States. I have joined a couple of traveling single groups and enjoy taking a break in a rest area in the middle of nowhere and hear someone calling my name. It makes me feel fantastic to know I am doing this myself with no help from anyone. Every day is exciting because I don't know where I will be going, what I will be doing, and whom I will meet. Not enough days in the year to do everything. See you down the road.

*Barbara Cormack, sixty years old, has one son and two daughters, ranging in age from twenty-four to thirty-six. She was married for thirty years to the most wonderful man she has ever known and has been a widow for five years. Barbara lives in Ontario, Canada, just north of Toronto. Barbara also contributed "The Mouse" and "Singing Wind Bookshop."*

*When one teeny-tiny foot bone out of twenty-six got broken,*
*Joei learned she could rely on the*
*kindness of strangers.*

# Agony of De-Feet

Joei Carlton Hossack

THERE ARE TWENTY-SIX BONES IN THE HUMAN FOOT. IT IS absolutely amazing how much it hurts to break just one of them. Even one of the teeny-tiny ones located on the side of the foot.

I pulled into a Good Sam campground in Gananoque, Ontario, after having driven farther than I had intended to on a hot muggy day in August. I paid for one night, which was how long I planned on staying. I was on my way to visit my family in Montreal, whom I had not seen in a couple of years. I pulled into my spot for the night. I connected my electricity. I immediately turned on my refrigerator since it was about 95 degrees and went back outside with my water hose. While returning from connecting my water hose, half my foot found the ridge that ran along-side my camper. Half my foot did not.

I wanted to scream. I stood there for a second, letting the pain sub-side. I hobbled over to the picnic table and watched as a large, blue egg developed on the outside of my left foot. I hobbled up the stairs to my camper and retrieved an ice pack. It didn't work. I limped over to the office.

She sat me down. She put a bag of ice against my swollen foot, and I gradually stopped whimpering as the pain subsided. I looked at it every few minutes. When it was frozen solid, it felt a whole lot better.

"Do you want to go to the hospital?" she asked giving me a puppy-dog look.

"It can't be broken," I said. "I wouldn't be able to walk on it if it were broken."

"Do you want to go to the hospital?" she asked again.

"Will someone be able to take me and bring me back?" I asked, not having a clue as to how far the hospital was or in which direction. The fact that it was getting on towards evening concerned me as well.

"I'll call Rose," she said and before I could really make up my mind, made the call. "Can you wait about ten minutes?" she asked. "They are in the middle of dinner."

Within minutes the door to the office opened and neatly dressed, freshly quaffed, lipsticked Rose poked her head into the office to see what probably appeared to her to be a geriatric ragamuffin. My eyes were burning red fighting off the tears. My T-shirt clung to me from the high heat and humidity and the sweat of pain. My sandals lay in a mini-heap by the bag of ice.

"Ready to go?" she asked.

"Could you drive me back to my camper and I'll get my purse. I really don't know if I should be going," I answered. "Doesn't feel too bad now."

"Better to be safe than sorry. Let's go anyway. It'll ease your mind," she said.

Without the ice keeping it frozen, I watched it swell again even though it had never really subsided. "Doesn't hurt much," I volunteered as I slowly wiggled my toes while sitting in the car. "I'm sure it's not broken."

The hospital in Brockville, Ontario, was thirty-five miles away. Rose knew exactly where it was since she has lived in the area all her life. She dropped me off at Emergency and went to park the car. I hobbled in. It was after seven and getting dark.

I told the receptionist my story. She filled out the necessary paperwork. Rose returned and we waited.

It seemed to take forever. They finally came and got me with a wheelchair. I was wheeled into X-ray and chided myself because I knew it couldn't be broken and I was wasting everyone's time.

My foot hurt each time the technician moved it to take an X-ray. I was returned to the hallway where Rose waited patiently.

"You haven't eaten yet," she said. "Would you like me to go get you something?" she asked.

"No," I answered, "perhaps when this is over we can grab something nearby. I'm so sorry about wasting your time," I said. "They're probably going to slap on an Ace bandage and send me home,"

Another hour went by before Rose and I found ourselves in one of the examining rooms. We chitchatted. Nurses came in and went out. The doctor will be in shortly to read your X-ray, I was told by one. One nurse came in with a bucket of water and strips of funny looking cloth on a silver cart. My immediate thought was that they needed the room for storage. Talk about living in Fantasyland.

During the evening I had been joking with one of the orderlies. He then came in and advised me that I was getting an "asskicking cast."

"Yours is going to be the first one I kick," I announced. "Are you telling me that it's broken?" I asked in disbelief.

"You'll have to wait for the doctor," he said.

Well, to make a long story short, it was broken. To cast or not to cast was left up to me. With a heavy heat wave and an air conditioner on the fritz I chose "no cast." It was one of those little bones that will heal with or without a cast, but I would have to be really, really careful. I got my Ace bandage and a prescription for Naprosyn, a painkiller with an anti-inflammatory. Rose walked the many blocks to where the car was parked and returned to pick me up at the door. She offered to wheel me outside in the wheelchair, but I walked out under my own steam. It was now after nine-thirty and we had to find an open drugstore. We found one. Rose waited the twenty minutes for the prescription to be filled. We stopped at Tim Horton's for a bite to eat. I was starving. I took a pill.

We arrived back at the campground just as they were closing the gate at eleven. Rose's husband was waiting for us. They helped me into my camper. I didn't lock the door that night—just in case. I slept like the dead.

Rose came by the next morning to see if there was anything I needed. She also explained that everyone in charge and especially her husband had been worried . . . not so much about me but about Rose. They had sent this lovely lady off with a total stranger. I could have been some maniac. I could have been some deviate with mayhem on my mind. As each hour passed they became more and more concerned and for a split second thought they might call the hospital or the police.

I stayed another day. I thanked Rose with an autographed copy of my book, *Everyone's Dream Everyone's Nightmare,* and a bookmark to make up for the gas she used getting me to and from.

A thousand blessings on Rosemary Burgess. It is because of people like Rose that I feel safe in traveling solo around North America. I don't know what I would have done without her.

*Joei Carlton Hossack, a full-time, solo RVer, is the author of* Everyone's Dream Everyone's Nightmare; Kiss This Florida, I'm Outta Here; A Million Miles From Home; Alaska Bound and Gagged; Free Spirit, Born to Wander; *and* Chasing The Lost Dream. *All six books are available through Amazon.com or http://www.JoeiCarlton.com. Joei also contributed "A Fine Bit of Madness."*

# Side Roads

### THE DUMP BY LINDA WILLARD

According to Murphy's Law it was time for something important to break. And it did, as soon as I'd settled into the campground and emptied the black tank. The little plastic holder that had so thoughtfully held the lever in place for twenty-two years suddenly broke off in my hand. My first thought was, "I can't use this toilet anymore because the lever is critical." Without it, the raw sewage would run right out on the ground.

I tried to survey the critical situation by feeling around underneath. If I could find a piece of wire, somehow I might be able to rig something up to hold the lever. No wire. Maybe a long shoelace? No shoelace. Wait a minute. A bungee cord! Of course, all RVers travel with bungee cords.

I wrapped, tightened, and pulled the ends together. Success. It held and didn't appear to leak. Once again, a problem solved using what's on hand. (But, just in case, I set the trusty pail underneath.)

### NO REGRETS BY HOPE SYKES

When I drove away from what was to have been my new home, I didn't have any real regrets. It just didn't feel right, but the open road did. Most everything that I owned merely went back into storage and I pointed the truck west by northwest seeking Outback America.

### SCARIEST MOMENT BY BARBARA CORMACK

My scariest moment on the road was having food poisoning in the Rio Grande Valley in Texas, in the hospital for five days, with no family or friends around.

*The open road, with its twists and turns, is a metaphor for
life. In retrospect, Carol Ann can see where one
turn took her away from her dreams.*

# Wrong Turn

## Carol Ann Sutherland

FOUR AND A HALF YEARS AGO, I LEFT MY HUSBAND AND
marriage of thirteen years, put all my worldly belongings in storage, bought
a 29-foot travel trailer, and headed south from northern British Columbia. No job in sight, not a great deal of money in the bank, just a very real
dream of working and traveling. There was so much I wanted to do and
see. I had no definite plans, no set direction, just a feeling of relief and
anticipation. I knew what I had been doing was wrong for me, as if who
I was, was fading and I felt that I wouldn't survive if I didn't get out into
the world, and fast—changes had to be made.

I did have an airline ticket in my pocket for Central America, dated
January 3, 1998—five months in the future. Another dream I was fulfilling.

Today, here I sit in a two-bedroom mortgaged condo, fully furnished,
a leased car in the underground parking lot, my travel trailer long sold,
and Central America a dim memory. A high-stress job hovers over me
like a vulture waiting to strike. My nights are sleepless, waking every hour,
reliving the day before, or worrying about the days to come. Where did I
make the wrong turn?

I can almost recall the exact day when a former employer phoned me about a management position they needed filling, asking me if I would apply?"

"No," was my first response. "I only want contract work, nothing full-time."

"This job was made for you, would you reconsider?"

"No, I can't, I have a ticket for Central America in January. I won't cancel."

"Would you consider canceling it if the terms were right?"

"No, I am going backpacking throughout Central America for three months with my kids and can't change my plans."

"Okay, if we give you a three-month leave of absence would you consider taking the job?" What could I say? Maybe I should have responded differently, but I decided to say yes and a turn in my life was made—left.

My dreams of working and traveling have been pushed aside for property ownership, pension building, stability, and a sense of family relief. Do I regret my decision? No, I just wish I had taken the good from it and not let it take over my life completely. I wish I had only compromised and not given up my dreams, only delayed them a short time.

Compromise. How could I have done that? Well, I could have taken the job offered, kept living in my travel trailer, saved my money, and got back on the road that much faster. Did I need the new living room furniture? No, I could have continued to borrow my son's futon. Was that new car necessary? No, but if I am to take business trips for my employer, I needed a reliable vehicle to drive over the winter roads. Was it necessary to buy a condo? No, but my parents sure felt a sense of relief when they saw me settle down. They could see me doing well in my career, having a nice home, and setting a good example for my grown-up kids.

And for a couple of years I went along with it, but today as I fill the water bottle to feed my thirsty plants, I feel a sense of loneliness that can only be felt when one aches with lost dreams and a sense of hopelessness. What is in my future? Will I continue to live my life for others and as they think I should? Or will I make a right turn in the near future and put myself back on the path towards my goal of working and living on the road, experiencing life as I wish to live it?

Time will tell. But I do have to remember I was the one who, at a crossroads in my life, made that turn, no one else, so I will have to be the one to look at a map, set a heading, and turn the wheels into another direction if I choose.

*Carol Ann Sutherland lives and works in Vancouver, British Columbia, sharing her home with two goldfish and a roomful of plants. She is currently working on a book for Canadian RVers. She recently bought a camper van—enabling her to travel on her own terms, even if it is only on weekends.*

*Never having driven their motorhome, Donna was in a quandary
after her husband's death. How could she continue the
RV lifestyle when she was afraid to drive?*

# To RV or Not

Donna Sauter

WE'D BEEN FULL-TIME RVING FOR SEVEN YEARS WHEN MY WORLD
fell apart. My husband of forty-four years died of leukemia the spring of
1997, leaving me with a 26-foot Itasca Class C motorhome that I'd never
driven. Why? Too scared to try.

I now lived in a 12' x 60' mobile home, missing my RV way of life as
well as my Charlie. When the numbness eased, I knew that for my own
piece of mind I had to buy a smaller motorhome, one that I felt I could
handle. I needed to prove to myself that I didn't have to give up the RV
lifestyle altogether.

My brother-in-law and his wife offered to help me find the RIGHT
motorhome. A cousin spotted one he thought might be good for me, so
off we went to check out the wee 1986 20-foot Coachmen micro-mini in
excellent condition. I knew it had to be mine. I was proud of it and me.
The salesman delivered it and when I saw it in my own yard, I panicked.
Good grief, what had I done? It didn't look like such a "wee" motorhome
any more.

Soon it came time for the maiden voyage. Our daughter Bonnie
agreed to go with me to Old Mill Marina RV Resort in Garibaldi, on the

northern coast of Oregon. The RV was packed and suddenly I was sitting in the driver's seat. I was numb, not ready to tackle Portland's many freeways that finally lead to Oregon's coast. I'm afraid of getting on freeways in a car, so how was I to drive this RV to get us safely to the coast? I begged Bonnie to drive the first freeway, but she wisely and firmly said, "No."

Before I had time to think, I was on the freeway. I remember saying, "Hang on, here we go." I was driving, changing lanes, making my way to the coast. Me! To my amazement, the RV stayed in the lanes and followed along just fine.

We found our site and busied ourselves with the hookups. I needed help with the sewer hookup since the lever to open the line was pointed inward under the rig, and I didn't have the strength to pull it. A security guard was kind enough to heed my call of distress. After that, Bonnie and I were proud of ourselves for having mastered the lights and water, only to find when we got inside that we had neither. To our embarrassment, we had forgotten to turn on the main power switch and the water faucet outside.

The next morning I drove northward to Nehalem to meet friends for breakfast. Now, all I had to worry about was backtracking the route we had come and return home.

I did it! I had taken the first step and was still an RVer. Although no longer a full-timer, I had proved I could go and come in my wee Coachmen any time I chose. I discovered that almost anything is possible, if you just try.

*Donna Sauter was married for forty-four years to Charles. They have a daughter Bonnie, son-in-law John, and two granddaughters. At one time she owned The Bookshelf on the Oregon Coast. Widowed in 1997, she married Elmer in 2001 and is "twice blessed." Donna also contributed "Two Harbors, Minnesota."*

# Exit Ramp

## WHAT I WISH I HADN'T BROUGHT BUT DID:

✐ anything I brought with me and wish I hadn't has long ago been tossed. *JL*

✐ too many dress up clothes and my sewing machine. I didn't even have it out of the box. *BC*

✐ all my junk. *SE*

✐ a lovely iron and ironing board I left at a thrift store in Arizona, donated after not using them for over a year. *MS*

✐ makeup, high heels, and an iron. What was I thinking! *NA*

✐ as many clothes. *AF*

✐ my sewing machine. I hate to sew with a machine, so after eight and a half years of carrying it along I am going to get rid of it. *SB*

✐ decorative things to hang on the walls and dust collectors. *LE*

✐ too many T-shirts. *DE*

✐ dress clothes. *CC*

✐ clothes—you simply don't need closets full of clothes. *DS*

✐ whatever it was, we got rid of it long ago. *JA*

✐ my fearing and worrying about the unknown. I admire travelers who have a risk-taking attitude about travel. *DW*

# Heart Places

------------------------------------------------

*Sometimes in your travels you find a place that is special. Perhaps the sights, sounds, and smells evoke a childhood memory, the music touches a chord, or the natural beauty overwhelms the senses. Or perhaps the people take you into the community like one of their own. In the following essays, our writers share what is special about a place that has touched their hearts.*

*Wild Latin colors, Spanish-style haciendas, and cobblestone streets
make this town special. But it is the gardens that make
San Miguel de Allende DeAnna's heart place.*

# San Miguel
# de Allende

- - - - - - - - - - - - - - - - - - - - - - - - - -

### DeAnna White

AS WE DROVE OUR RV ACROSS THE BORDER, A MAGICAL LINE
was crossed. The sights, sounds, and smells were foreign as we immersed
ourselves into a new language and an exotic Latin culture. After several
months traveling throughout Mexico, we began missing newspapers, cultural activities, and other English-speaking travelers. Then we discovered
San Miguel de Allende, located in the mountains north of Mexico City.
Here we found the perfect blend of culture and ambience.

A sizable colony of American students, artists, and pensioners has
put its stamp on this charming city. They enjoy the largest English language library in Mexico and a weekly English paper filled with cultural
and community events. The paper lists theater productions, art openings
at galleries, the weekly markets, and concerts.

We stayed two months on our first visit to San Miguel. I remember
tastes of mango and coconut ices, smells of roasting chicken in the streets,
and wild Latin colors. Yet it is the gardens that make me yearn for my
heart place. I discovered a high desert botanical garden, with cacti unique
to Mexico. My favorite find was an old saddle factory that is now used to
display a magnificent orchid collection. We climbed a long cobblestone

hill at the edge of town to reach the converted factory building. I knocked and the caretaker admitted us. The door opened into a tiered courtyard overflowing with flowers and a spectacular view of the hills of San Miguel.

People wake up early in San Miguel. The bells of the churches clang in the crisp still morning air. At an altitude of 6000 feet, the temperature is perfect in this colonial city in Mexico. Silver mining in the boom days financed remarkable architecture with cobblestone streets. It is a city of Spanish-style haciendas with their massive doors and walls. Bougainvillea blossoms cover the white and pastel-shaded walls. We stayed at the La Siesta RV campground, within a twenty-minute walk from the center of the town.

Traveling alone in a strange city normally intimidates me. But here I was comfortable and felt safe walking through the streets during the day. One time I decided to attend a concert at night alone. The streets were alive with families enjoying the nightlife. After the performance, I wandered into the city square. The night bubbled with activity. People ate and drank at the sidewalk cafes, gossiping with neighbors. Even a bit of formal courtship was going on as the teens walked back and forth through the promenade. Music filled the streets as mariachis serenaded in the distance. I was a woman alone, enjoying the feeling of safety and freedom to be by myself. Magical San Miguel became a heart place for me that night. It beckons my return.

*DeAnna White also contributed "Women's Friendships."*

# Scenic Overlooks

### BLACK HILLS OF SOUTH DAKOTA BY JOANNE ALEXAKIS

I love the Hills. The terrain is all ups and downs. Ridges, valleys, peaks, draws, buttes, and gullies make up this lofty and lowland scenery. Narrow curvy roads (enough to show a flatlander what "white-knuckle driving" is all about) carry you through the countryside. Stands of ponderosa pine are so thick that from a distance they make the hillsides appear dark—almost black.

Scratch and sniff a ponderosa tree trunk, and you catch the scent of butterscotch. I love the big, unhazy, ocean-blue skies. Towering, bright, white, puffy clouds waft by in the toasty warmth of the sun. Tumultuous darkening clouds scudding along can signal tremendous thunderstorms of lightning, wind, rain, and hail. Wild tempestuous weather comes into the Hills quickly and leaves just as fast. The air is not humid. Your sandwich bread can dry out before you finish eating it.

Visitors to the beautiful Black Hills of South Dakota bring smiles and hopes for a refreshing and relaxing vacation. Being here brings my heart back home.

### MORAINE LAKE BY JANET R. WILDER

There are places in this world where one is certain a finger of the hand of God has touched the earth. Moraine Lake in Lake Louise National Park, Alberta, Canada, is such a place. The opaque turquoise water, gleaming like a bright jewel in the summer sun, reflects the high peaks of the Canadian Rockies that surround it. Near the shore is an enormous pile of rocks, a miniature mountain, whose origin is a geological mystery. Visitors follow a path up the rock pile to the top. As the path wends upwards, the vistas change and each view of Moraine Lake and the surrounding mountains grabs your heart and catches your breath. A cloak of serenity drapes itself about your shoulders. Rest on the bench near the top; spend a few moments gazing at the gem-brilliant lake and contemplate its Divine source.

*Celebrating her coming sixtieth birthday, Sharlene rafted down*
*the mighty Yukon River. Although she declined to use goose*
*poop on her lips as her guide had recommended,*
*together the two of them successfully paddled*
*five hundred miles in fourteen days.*

# The Mighty
# Yukon River

- - - - - - - - - - - - - - - - - - - - - - - - - - - - -

### Sharlene Minshall

THE SIGN BECKONED, "RAFT THROUGH UNTOUCHED ALASKAN wilderness." Bill Elmore, forty-six, former North Slope crane operator, jack-of-all-trades, and guide, didn't laugh when I poured out my soul's desire. "I want to canoe the mighty Yukon River. I want to experience the wilderness. I want to pit myself against nature." What I really wanted to do was erase his look that said, "This woman is a nut case."

This stretch of the Yukon had no rapids, but I knew hypothermia would likely claim our lives if storms or any wrong moves dumped us in the middle of the often mile-wide river. I knew grizzlies were a danger, bugs would be annoying, and if either of us became incapacitated, we were isolated from civilization. But, I didn't realize how much trouble I was in until Bill announced, "We'll have to average paddling forty miles a day." I still managed a resounding "Yessss!"

Our "bare bones" equipment included food, one waterproof bag each for personal gear, a tent, poles, sleeping bags, pads, tarp and topographical maps, packed between two lawn chairs (a stroke of comfort genius) in a seventeen-foot canoe. Daypacks held immediate necessities. We wore lifejackets and had water sippers handy to stay properly hydrated.

On May 31, we left Eagle, Alaska, with icebergs still jammed into the riverbanks. A storm appeared frighteningly fast before noon. We were more concerned with double-time paddling to shore than digging out rain gear. It passed as quickly as it came.

My excitement was beyond description—for the first thirty miles. At thirty-five miles, my eyes glazed over. At forty miles we stopped for the night. Since I had agreed with unbounded enthusiasm to share the work, Bill wound me up and I automatically carried gear and supplies to the sandbar. I didn't feel tired; I couldn't feel. My arms had dropped off at thirty-eight miles.

A hot meal hand-dipped into my mouth by a sympathetic guide renewed my strength. If I had any doubts about his wilderness camping ability, they disappeared when he balanced a time-honored and fire-blackened kettle on the burning logs to heat water.

As we paddled through the Yukon-Charley Rivers National Preserve, we explored hundred-year-old cabins with sod roofs. Doors were unlocked for anyone who needed shelter. We hiked up Coal Creek to pan for gold. This left us wealthy beyond measure, not with gold, but in the beauty of a perfect crisp, spring morning.

Bill had never guided beyond Circle, Alaska. We paddled through the unknown waters of the Yukon Flats National Wildlife Refuge, sometimes twenty miles wide with lakes and islands. Despite topo maps, we couldn't judge where we were. Only once were we fooled into a slough. The canoe mired in mud. Bill said, "We may have to get out and pull."

I said, "What do you mean 'we,' hired guide?" We muscled our way out and found the main channel five miles downstream, passing over the Arctic Circle with nary a bump.

Logs floated into convenient stacks on the island sandbars where we sought nightly and break-time refuge. We built fires on the river's edge, the ashes to be washed away in the next storm. No one would know we had been there. We washed our dishes and bathed in Yukon River water. Clear water streams provided drinking water, after Giardia lamblia boiled away.

The days began with bravado. I shouted into the sky, "Good Morning God, Hello World" and the first chorus of Oh, What a Beautiful Morning. A quiet voice behind me said, "Now you know why we aren't seeing many animals."

When the wind whipped wide-open spaces into whitewater and sand blew across the islands, we exited the river or paddled within ten feet of shore. We frequently stopped for "arm" breaks or found dry spots on the riverbank, curled up, and snoozed for five or ten minutes. When the water was glassy-smooth, we lay back and let the current turn the canoe in lazy circles under magnificent blue skies and billowy clouds.

Except for going after mosquitoes with his 44, Bill was a laid-back kind of guy. He had sworn to protect my life for two weeks in the wilderness. He said confrontation with a bear or moose was unlikely, but to his credit, he defended me from an extraordinary amount of tracks. Before each meal, Bill gave thanks to God for our safety and good health. After several days of our combined gourmet cooking, it was considered in our best interests to continue.

It was truly amazing that two strangers got on so well, but I had to be careful following his advice. In the land of two million migrating geese, he said, "Use goose poop on your lips so you aren't tempted to lick them and cause chapping." With the advent of mosquitoes, I leave you with my own profound piece of wilderness camping advice, "If you moon a mosquito, repellent is the bottom line for comfort."

One wind-laden day when we had paddled only fifteen miles, we agreed the first one to awaken would check the river. If it was smooth, we would get an early start. I awakened at 2:30 a.m. The water was smooth as pudding. With caution the better part of valor, I tapped Bill's sleeping bag with the gun next to it. True to his word, we were on the river by 3 a.m. Although the sun had barely dipped to the horizon, we watched it pop back over snow-covered mountains, a magnificent day on the Yukon. We paddled sixty-three miles that day. During a slack time, I noticed Bill scribbling furiously, rewording future contracts, "There will be no paddling before my time."

All too soon we rounded a bend and saw the silver Trans-Alaska Pipeline ahead of us. We floated quietly the last few minutes, knowing our peaceful world would soon to be assaulted by "The Outside." We pulled out at the Yukon River Bridge at the Dalton Highway, 500 miles and 14 days wiser. My terrific guide gave me a big hug and said, "We did it. I'm proud of you."

It was the adventure of a lifetime and a great way to celebrate a coming sixtieth birthday. God bless.


This is a condensation of a story taken from the completely revised 2002 edition of *RVing Alaska and Canada*. This "How-to" and "Why-not" book, that combines humor, information, and adventure, is available through her Web site or direct from the author, Sharlene Minshall, c/o Gypsy Press (web), P.O. Box 1040, Congress, AZ 85332-1040 for $16.95. Postage and Handling $4 one book, $1 additional books. Check "Charlie's" Web page for the list of her other books and to place an order. http://www.Full-time-rver.com.


*A former medical secretary, Sharlene "Charlie" Minshall was a "vacation-time" RVer for twenty years before the death of her husband. Nearly seventeen years and 300,000 miles of full-time solo RVing have taken her from her home state of Michigan to adventures in fifty United and seventeen Mexican States, and all Canadian Provinces and Territories (except Nunavut). She has two daughters and two grandchildren. Charlie is a freelance writer, columnist, author of six RV-related books, and has been a Life on Wheels instructor since 1996.*

# Scenic Overlooks

### WOODSTOCK, VERMONT BY MYRNA COURTNEY

When we first drove into Woodstock, Vermont, I had the uncanny feeling that I had been there before, which I had not. I knew which way to turn to go into town and that an old-time hardware store would lie around the next corner. I recognized a building front done in rich, deep greens and brass. I knew which café served the best food and where it was. Perhaps all this was because many quaint New England towns are laid out in similar fashion. Perhaps it was the autumnal glory that surrounded us, the locals in sweaters and corduroy on their errands, the smoky smell of the air. Something about the place gave me an immediate, familiar peacefulness.

We visited friends in their two hundred-year-old farmhouse with a walk-in kitchen fireplace as well as fifteen others, one to each room. Indian shutters. White rail fences running along both sides of the lane. A wonderful old horse barn. A pond lined with maples, gold and red. I stepped to one side to see the back roof of the house, knowing there would be a weather vane there, but perhaps it was because lots of old New England houses have weather vanes. I walked alone in the pasture, kicking leaves and gazing at the sky as a true Vermonter would do, but perhaps it was because I've seen New Englanders do that in movies. I sat on the cobblestone courtyard with the resident collie poking his fine head under my booted toe for a good rub and felt as if I were in another time. But perhaps it was because I wanted to be. Or, perhaps, I had been.

### MOST BEAUTIFUL PLACE BY DONNA ELLIS

Picture saguaro, organ pipe, and cholla cacti at night with a full moon or during a rare rainstorm. You are in the middle of the Sonoran Desert in southern Arizona, the most beautiful place in the world.

*Each place has its special magic. For Stephanie, the
magic of Newfoundland was in its music
and friendly people.*

# Magical
# Newfoundland
--------------------------------------

## Stephanie Bernhagen

AS WE HEADED NORTH FROM CHANNEL-PORT-AUX-BASQUE,
Newfoundland, I was awestruck by the beauty. We were greeted by rolling green foothills with grayish-white boulders scattered everywhere. In
the dips and valleys were bogs and ponds. Suddenly the foothills pushed
back to the east as mountains strained to reach the sky. A valley of streams
lay between the mountains and us. To the west, ocean waves slapped
against the sandy beaches. I was hooked.

The camping season is short this far north, so there are few campgrounds. Most RVers find themselves boondocking in gravel pits along
the road for at least part of their trip. When near a town the entire community seems to come out and drive by to see the big rigs from the United
States. The few RVs in Newfoundland are small Class Cs.

Hiking trails are typically boardwalks over boggy land. One day we
drove to Kings Point, where we found a wonderful hiking trail that was
under construction. The trail started out as a boardwalk, but before long
we found ourselves walking a dirt path that had been dug down eighteen
inches in preparation for more boardwalk. Next we balanced ourselves on
small logs as we crossed bogs, hiking the original trail. "Wow, it takes a
lot to build a trail like this," we realized.

We left a message for friends telling them about the trail, which had water, dump, and plenty of room for their RVs. Arriving at Kings Point a few days later, they had no sooner gotten their rigs parked when the entire town—including the mayor and tourism director—came out to welcome them. Apparently few RVs came down the rough road to visit Kings Point. Later that evening one of the men stopped by one of the rigs with Texas license plates. He knocked at the door, saying, "My son has never met Texans."

We spent a few nights in Twillingate, just one of many towns with magical names like Leading Tickles, Tizzard's Harbour, and Ferryland. In Twillingate we found the magic of Newfoundland's music. A combination of fiddle, accordion, hand drum, and ugly stick combined to bring us a new high. What's an ugly stick you ask? Take an old broom handle and replace the broom with an old boot or tennis shoe. Place a tomato juice can, with bells in it, on the top of the stick. Paint a face and put some hair on the can. Drive nails in the stick holding several beer bottle tops each. Next, take a short, hand-held stick and cut notches in it. Now stomp that ugly stick up and down while rubbing the short, notched stick back and forth on the ugly stick and listen as the music magically comes to life.

We attended a couple of provincial festivals, called Soirées and continued to experience the magic of the music. At Kelligrew we stopped at a small strip mall a couple blocks from where the Soirée would be and asked if we could stay in their parking lot. "Certainly! We will just call the Soirée planners and let them know not to chase you off." That night, three communities over, we stopped at the visitor's center and asked about the Soirée events. One thing led to another and they said, "Oh, you are the ones parked at the mall in Kelligrew." We felt like part of the community.

One of our favorite stops was at Cape St. Mary, home of the birds. From a green oceanside bluff, we watched the birds in their own habitat. The largest cluster roosted on a rock outcropping a few feet from the bluff. Mothers cared for the young while some birds played childish games, pushing others from their ledge on the outcropping. It makes one realize how complex a bird's life is.

With two nights left, we headed from St. Bride's to Argentia to catch the long ferry back to Nova Scotia. No one had warned us that Highway 100 had six valleys and therefore six mountains to climb along the way. Had these been 6 percent grades it would have been one thing, but they were 15-20 percent grades! One of the motorhomes we traveled with had no problems, the second overheated their brakes, and we had to stop to cool our transmission. Since there was no shoulder, we sat in the middle of the road atop one of these mountains. Three cars passed us and all three stopped to ask if we needed assistance.

As we started up the next steep mountainside, we heard a noise that demanded we stop and check it. It wasn't long before an entire family, including the dogs, had joined us alongside the road. The father asked if there was anything he could do to help and crawled under the truck with Paul. It turned out the noise was from a piece of electrical tape on the tire flapping against the sidewall. Whew.

That night we obtained the grocery store manager's blessing to spend the night. Shortly afterwards there was a knock at the door. The gentleman asked, "Do you have any questions I can answer about the area?" We told him sadly our journey was ending and that we would be taking the ferry back the next day. He said he just wanted to make sure we knew what there was to see in the area.

The people of this large island were some of the friendliest and most helpful I have ever met. And the beauty was a combination of *National Geographic* and fairytales. The music moved me as no other music has. Newfoundland showed me I could still experience magic as a child does.

*Stephanie and husband Paul were in their 30s when they hit the road in 1994. Stephanie's book,* Take Back Your Life! Travel Full-Time in an RV, *has helped educate RVers and wannabes about the RV lifestyle. New experiences, the wonderful people she meets, and volunteering in the communities she visits are what make the lifestyle so special. Stephanie also contributed "A Surprise."*

# Scenic Overlooks

## NORTHERN MINNESOTA BY NAN AMANN

My heart place is still from childhood and makes no adult sense, but so many things don't. It is any of the serene, clear cold lakes in northern Minnesota, near Beltrami or Bemidji. The feeling of total escape and vacation comes immediately when driving on those little gravelly roads and finally arriving at one of the many cabins there. The pines, maples, and birch trees line up and wave their leaves in greeting. The lakes shimmer in the quiet heat, reflecting the blues of the cloudless sky. Fish hide in the rushes just across the lake waiting for me. There is no noise other than the breeze playing quietly in the trees. Occasionally a bird quarrels with a neighbor. The water is icy cold. The beer is icy cold and the rowboat rocks gently as I slip a line in the water.

Forget the mosquitoes and bomber-sized horse flies, forget the leeches that attach themselves creepily when you swim. Forget the huge storms that spring up from nowhere, with gale-force winds throwing hail and rain. Forget the chill blast of winter that bites with vengeance, and forget that natives wear shorts when the temperature is fifty because they consider that a heat wave. Just loll in a lawn chair listening for the loons and waiting for the giant stars that are close enough to touch. When I need "home," I close my eyes and I am there.

## CAPE BRETON ISLE BY CINDY COOK

It's hard to describe the feeling I had in Cape Breton. It was really like another country. It had some of the nicest people I've met anywhere. The landscape was fresh, billboardless, dotted with simple houses, laundry hanging on a line out back. Small signs everywhere quietly advertising Scotsburn ice cream. I'm going to look at the map and think about going back next summer!

*The rules prohibit smoking, drinking, glass containers, and bathing suits. What, no bathing suits? Sally, from the bundled-up climes of Canada, finds community and her heart place in the hot springs.*

# Tecopa Hot Springs

### Sally Banks

DESERT HOT SPRINGS. AN ODD COMBINATION. WHO'D WANT TO soak in hot water in this parched land? It's rather like carrying coals to Newcastle or taking a busman's holiday. Where's the sense in that? But hundreds of people do just that every day in this dusty little California outpost. And they travel great distances to do it.

At first glance the hot springs are not an enticing sight. The buildings—one for women, one for men—look old and shabby, sun-bleached and peeling after squatting for decades in the desert heat. The concrete pools themselves, one hot and one slightly cooler, are small, with only enough room for eight or nine people at a time.

Just across the road, at the Inyo County office, you can pick up a copy of "Bathhouse Rules & Regulations." They are explicit. DO NOT take articles of value into the bathhouses . . . Smoking IS NOT permitted . . . Intoxicated individuals ARE NOT permitted . . . Food or beverages ARE NOT permitted . . . Glass IS NOT permitted . . . Bathing suits or clothing of any kind ARE NOT to be worn in the baths.

Whoa. What's this? Nude bathing? Nude is fine for baby pictures but not something normal adults engage in. We live in a society conditioned by culture and religion to cover up. Except if you're trying to market clothing, cars, makeup, movies, magazines, cigarettes, alcohol, and anything else where sex helps make a sale. In that case, seductive clothing—or none at all—is par for the course.

But to take your clothes off? In public? In front of complete strangers? The mere thought makes many women choke. Especially women who are no longer—if they ever were—slender, trim, taut-tummied, and wrinkle-free. If you come to the baths, there's no place to hide. All you're left wearing is some jewelry and a nervous smile. Stretch marks. Varicose veins. Folds of fat and cellulite. Scars, bruises, a missing breast. They're present for all the world to see—or at least that small part sharing the pool with you.

But you know what? After the first few terrifying minutes, it doesn't matter. Nude bathing is not about sensuality or looking good. It's about learning to shed inhibitions and preconceived ideas about ourselves and others along with our clothes.

Our group, a varied collection of RVers, is boondocking on the desert. We range in age from early 40s to late 60s. Some know each other well and are keen "hot springers." Others are first-timers, uncertain of the situation they have found themselves in.

The water has a way of bringing out stories. From discussions of beading and tomorrow's potluck preparations and where we're traveling to next, we wander into tales of how we met our spouses, of what it's like to live so close with someone in a tin can on wheels, or of how life changes when a beloved partner dies. Some tell of abusive relationships, of children gone wrong, of aging parents.

And all the time the water is weaving its magic, soothing, calming, reassuring.

One day, we're joined by a flock of young birds who fly in, boisterous and noisy. They are the wives and girlfriends of the fellows racing ATVs over the nearby sand dunes. These young women chatter the whole time, of men and clothes and jobs and what's for supper. They leave as quickly as they came, and quiet settles over the pools again.

Another time we meet seven Japanese women in the baths. They've driven all the way from Los Angeles. They talk constantly and one splashes up and down the entire time. We try sign language for a few moments, then each group returns to its own words and ways.

One day a local woman—who was born and raised in Tecopa, moved away, then returned—shares her memories of the early days. She tells of the Indians and the origins of the pools. And just where the hot springs enter the pool and why the bottom is covered with small, rounded pebbles (to disperse the gasses trapped in the hot water bubbling up from the bottom of the pool).

You can visit the baths anytime. They're open seven days a week, twenty-four hours a day, except for the twice-weekly cleaning.

Some bathers come early each morning, a ritual for coaxing arthritic joints into movement. Others prefer mid-afternoon, to rinse off the day's dust under the shower and then let the water work out the kinks from a hike to China Ranch.

Come a little later and you can watch the sky turn from day to dusk, the palette of colors changing from blue to orange to mauve. On the rare occasions when it rains, you can catch cool drops on the hot skin of your forehead and cheeks.

Evening is my favorite time. The hot pool in the women's building has no roof so I have a wonderful view of the sky. The water, like liquid velvet, wraps you in its warm embrace. Sometimes a faint breeze flows over the lip of the building and finds its way down to pool level. Far above, in the darkness, millions of tiny jewels sparkle in the heavens.

This is a peaceful time, a time for reflection, for soft thoughts, for meditation. Or for nothing at all. And perhaps that's the wonder and the appeal of the pools. They are, like life, what we make of them.

Come on in. The water's fine.

*Sally Banks has been a freelance writer and editor for more than thirty years. Since Gerry put wheels under her heels, she's become a free spirit. They live in Alberta for six months of the year, then spend the winter in their fifth wheel, wandering though the American Southwest and Mexico.*

# Scenic Overlooks

TWO HARBORS, MINNESOTA BY DONNA SAUTER

The first time I saw Two Harbors, Minnesota, was the summer of 1995. From that time on, I yearned to visit there again. I've heard it said, "You can't go back again," but I was anxious to show this special place to my new husband. Elmer and I went there on our honeymoon, July 2001.

Thirty-five miles north of Duluth, Minnesota, along the western shore of Lake Superior, Two Harbors opens up from the lake. A cement walkable breakwater protrudes outward from the left side of the harbor, while docks line the right side. The Two Harbors lighthouse, "watching" from behind the breakwater, is a small picturesque brick structure. A nearby white house is used as the gift shop.

On the townside of the harbor lies a paved parking area and public boat ramps. I enjoy the manicured lawns lining the left shoreline and the cement tables and benches. I've sat for hours watching an ore boat (six hundred- to eight hundred-feet long) as it slips into the harbor without help of tugs. The boat slides close to the shoreline at the inside of the harbor, then slowly turns, easing up to the dock. Loading its cargo of taconite takes about eight hours.

A jut of land separates the harbor from where the RV park is located. A pathway with trees and views of Lake Superior make the mile walk to the harbor pleasurable.

The lighthouse is open to the public for tours. Private boats come in and out of the harbor. I even saw a couple of people snorkeling! An ore boat is either coming in, tied up at the dock, or leaving, most every day.

Even with those numerous activities, I found the sounds seemed to be swallowed up. As gulls search for tidbits of food, one can sit quietly, breathe the lake air, watch the shimmer of the sun and moonlight on the water, and be at peace with oneself.

Yes, I could go back. The town has grown, but beautiful Two Harbors, Minnesota, remains my heart place.

*One spot, an endless variety of views —*
*Cathi's heart place*

# Heart Place

- - - - - - - - - - - - - - - - - - - - - - - - - - - -

Cathi Tessier

THERE'S A SPECIAL PLACE I GO, A PLACE THAT'S JUST FOR ME. It's filled with the wondrous sights and sound of forest, desert, land, and sea.

It's a potpourri of many of my favorite things, colorful birds and flowers, sunshine and showers. Sights to inspire ideas and wake up my senses, to mull over yesterday's puzzlements and mend broken fences.

I can be found there early in the morning, watching the sun's rays peeking through the tallest evergreens, the natural beauty both compelling and serene, greeting and offering me a new day.

It's a place where dreams begin and sorrows fade. A place to find my daily solace, to purge and refresh, to lay aside sadness, to meditate and ponder, or just glance out yonder.

Wherever our travels take us I always return to my heart place. It's just a moment away, my retreat, a window to my world. My living room window is—my heart place.

*Cathi Tessier also contributed "City Girl Takes a Hike."*

# *Exit Ramp*

## FOR ME, BOONDOCKING IS . . .

✍ a great way to get away and see and experience places I couldn't otherwise. I enjoy it much more than RV parks where I can sit at my picnic table and watch my neighbor's TV at a high price. RV's are self-contained for a reason. *LE*

✍ our way of making ends meet. Finding a good boondocking spot is like discovering buried treasure. *MS*

✍ the perfect camping style for our self-sufficient house on wheels. Unplugging from the world, we enjoy our electrical stuff using solar. It makes us giddy to unhitch, turn off the engine, and listen to the music of the woods. *DW*

✍ freedom. *SB*

✍ one of the great joys of RVing. It's waking to the sound of desert birds, instead of your neighbour's furnace. It's a light breeze filled with the fragrance of mountain flowers, instead of diesel fumes. It's watching frogs and dragonflies, instead of towed cars and dogs on a leash. And it's falling asleep under starlight, instead of street lamps and neon signs. *SBanks*

✍ okay for about a week and one-half. I do like full hookups. *BC*

✍ absolutely wonderful . . . for a few days. Then I start longing for the park, the plug, the pool, the people, the potlucks. For a city girl like me, it's just too rugged and primitive. *CT*

✍ best if not done in a truck parking lot next to a dump. *NA*

✍ fun, as long as it's not a good TV night. *SE*

# The Last Word

----------------------------------------

*Traveling on the open road may give us different experiences than a more traditional life, but each life experience, no matter where it takes place, changes and shapes us. Our journeys not only take us to new places, but are also a metaphor for the growth and changes in our lives. Our stories connect us to each other and the larger community of women everywhere.*

*Long's Peak Challenge, our last story, epitomizes the journeys we all have taken. Climbing a 14,255-foot peak in Colorado is not for everyone, but as many of our authors have learned, meeting life's challenges, no matter what they are, strengthens us. So too for Jaimie as she confronts the physical and mental challenges of the climb.*

# Long's Peak Challenge

Jaimie Hall

MY ALARM RINGS AT 2 A.M. IT'S NOW OR NEVER. I DRESS, CHECK my pack. I need to be on the trail to climb Long's Peak by 3 a.m. so I can be headed down before the usual early afternoon thunderstorms. I park at the trailhead, elevation 9,500 feet, sign in, and at 2:50 start up the trail. I am carrying about twenty pounds—a gallon of water, rain gear, heavier clothes, plus plenty of food. Not eating and drinking enough can cause altitude sickness and fatigue.

The trail switchbacks through Goblin Forest. In the moonlight trees are transformed into creatures. I shift between excitement and assurance to wondering what I am doing here.

I emerge to cross treeless tundra to Chasm Lake Junction. Somewhere between there and the Boulder Field, I join a group of three hikers: two college-aged kids, Ty and Sarah, and a man about my age, Bill. We reach the Boulder Field as the sun rises, a red ball. The diamond face of Long's Peak looms before us. We have come 5.9 miles and are at 12,760 feet.

Frigid air whips over the mountain pass. I add clothing and take a bite of my frozen Power Bar. I remember the guidebook: the last 1.6 miles after the Boulder Field, with an elevation gain of 1,500 feet, is the toughest. We must climb around the mountain to the back side before making our final ascent.

The Boulder Field looms before us, a stretch of car-sized boulders. Jumping from boulder to boulder we gain another 500 feet. At the Keyhole, I am suddenly looking over a two-foot ledge—straight down 1,000 feet. The mountain completely drops away. Pushing fear back, I crawl to the left across the narrow ledge to the trail. Then we follow painted bull's-eyes, which will guide us along the rest of the trail to the top. We're in the shadow of the mountain, winding our way along a narrow trail. A ribbon of climbers stretches ahead.

Around yet another bend, we reach the "Trough," a path through loose rocks and stones at about a 35-degree angle. Now, at above 13,000 feet, every step is an effort. I stop to catch my breath every few steps. Ty is feeling light-headed. The Trough seems never-ending. Bill, traveling slowly, is hidden from our sight below. Finally after surmounting the last slippery rock with virtually no handholds, Sarah, Ty, and I climb through the hole in the skyline formed by two rocks.

We are thrust out into the sunshine on a ledge aptly called the "Narrows." The whole mountain drops straight down more than 2,000 feet from the skinny ledge we have to walk for the next quarter mile to the next edge of the mountain. A woman behind us sobs in sheer terror. "I'm scared too," I tell her. There are handholds on the rocks, in most places for both hands, in some, only on the cliff side. My pack rubs. I don't want to leave it, but what if it pushes me out too far over the ledge? Ty waits for Bill; Sarah and I go on. Holding on for dear life, we inch our way to the end of the Narrows. Nearing the end, we have to work our way around a small boulder, practically hanging out over the edge of the world. I focus totally on my feet and hands. We make it and collapse.

We turn and look up at the "Home Stretch." Climbers had made it sound like we'd be walking up a steep slope. WRONG. We see people crawling up a crack in the sheer rock wall. I want to turn back. I've never done any real climbing. Not when a mistake would be fatal. My pack throws my balance off slightly, making me more nervous. I am pushing questions out of my head about getting back down. If I think about that,

I'll never go on. Finally Sarah and I look at each other. We just do it. We follow the crack straight up the mountain. I turn off all thought, putting one hand and one foot in front of the other and look only that far in front of me.

11 a.m.: Exhausted, as much from terror as muscle fatigue and lack of oxygen, I am at the summit at 14,255 feet. A sob nearly escapes. I fight for control. I can't give in to emotion. I still have to get down. The top is about the size of a football field, covered with rocks. The sky is blue and clear and I can see practically forever. To the north is the historic Stanley Hotel in Estes Park where I am working this summer. To the east are the plains. We stand above neighboring mountains, stretching endlessly before us.

Bill and Ty arrive, we eat lunch, take pictures to commemorate the occasion, and sign the log. At least twenty other climbers share the summit with us. The woman who cried at the Narrows is there. I congratulate her.

As we rest, a woman explains she goes down on all "fives"—counting her butt. Her method becomes mine. Going down is even more of a strain on already exhausted legs and nerves. The world drops away before me. Thunder and Lion Lakes, mere dots, are more than 5,000 feet below. We make it down the Home Stretch.

Then back through the Narrows. The constant drop-away is nerve-wracking. My legs are shaky. My mind thinks "Stop," but I must keep going. I alone am responsible for getting myself down. At least breathing is easier now. With no thunderstorms looming, we aren't pressured by time.

The loose rocks in the Trough take constant vigilance. Stepping down strains already aching, tired leg muscles even more. Hands, sore from death grips on the rocks above, must be ready to grab hold at any moment. One step, then another.

Finally we are headed to the Keyhole. Incredibly, we are passed by five Mennonites. They carry no water or food. The two women wear tennis shoes, dresses, and light jackets. The men wear traditional clothes plus light jackets and baseball caps. They must have arrived at the top while we ate. They breeze by us, showing no signs of fatigue.

3 p.m.: We are back through the Boulder Field. We are taking frequent long breaks, longer than if I were alone. However, I feel a loyalty to my adopted hiking group for giving me moral support all this way. Only 5.9 miles. I will my legs and feet to keep moving. I know all about Ty's mountain biking adventures and plans to major in nursing in college. Bill is trying to mend relationships with his children, devastated by divorce. Sarah will soon head home to Minnesota to resume college.

Finally, we are back. It took us fifteen hours, longer than any of the other eighty climbers this day. Our sense of accomplishment is not dimmed by this fact.

As I look back, setting a goal, pushing my limits was the high. Facing danger, mastering emotions, and coming out unscathed is growth, no matter what the challenge. I am, in a sense, born anew. I have shed my current shell, much like a crab does, and emerged slightly enlarged. I carry the strength from this day within me forever.

*Jaimie Hall and her husband Bill sold everything and hit the road in 1992. They work about six months of the year, usually at national parks. In addition to co-editing this book, Jaimie authored* Support Your RV Lifestyle! An Insider's Guide to Working on the Road. *See http://www.rvhometown.com.*

# Glossary

*The authors of our stories use a number of terms common to those already participating in the RV lifestyle, but may be unfamiliar to a wider audience.*

**Blue tank:** Small portable container, usually 20-30 gallons, for emptying part of the holding tanks without having to move the rig.

**Black and gray water tanks:** Holding tanks for waste water from toilet (black) and from showers and sinks (gray).

**Boomers:** A large group of (mostly) pre-retirement age RVers who are members of an Escapees RV Club special interest group, Boomers.

**Boondocking:** Camping with no water, sewer, or power hookups.

**CARE Center:** A nonprofit corporation that provides a safe haven with professional assistance at affordable prices for Escapees RV Club members whose travels are permanently ended or temporarily interrupted because of health problems. Residents continue to live in their RVs.

**Class Cs:** Motorhomes with a conventional cab, usually with a bed over the cab.

**Dually:** A pickup truck with four wheels on the rear axle.

**Escapade:** An Escapees RV Club rally, held twice a year, which includes seminars, entertainment, food, and general socializing.

**Escapees RV Club:** RV organization that serves many purposes: Support ( providing venues for people of like interests to find each other, mail and other communication services, CARE); Knowledge (magazine, Escapade,

Web site); Parking (campgrounds that provide a permanent home base for travelers as well as a temporary stop). Members are referred to as "Escapees."

**Fifth wheel:** A trailer that hitches in the bed of a tow truck, unlike the travel trailer that hitches to the back of a truck.

**Full-time RVing:** The lifestyle of full-time RVers, who live and travel in their RV 365 days a year.

**Habitat for Humanity Care-A-Vanners:** A special subgroup of Habitat for Humanity where RVers come together across the country to build homes for those in need.

**Motorhome:** An RV where the driving compartment is within the RV.

**RV:** Recreational vehicle, from a small pop-up trailer to a million dollar luxury motorhome.

**RVers:** People who travel in their RV whether for a weekend, extended period of time, or full-time.

**SKPs:** Pronounced "skips," these are the members of the Escapees RV Club. When the word "Escapees" is said fast, it sounds like the letters, S-K-P, which stand for Support, Knowledge, Parking. It also stands for Special Kind of People. SKPs often greet each other with hugs.

**Toad:** The vehicle towed behind a motorhome.

**Winnie:** Nickname for Winnebago, a popular brand of motorhome.

**Workamper:** Phrase coined by *Workamper News* for RVers who combine all kinds of work with full- or part-time RV camping.

# Bios

THESE WOMEN CONTRIBUTED SHORT PIECES. THEIR BIOS ARE NOT INCLUDED ELSEWHERE:

Darlene Miller: Prior to becoming a full-time RVer in 1997, Darlene was a registered nurse, director of a day care center, wife, mother, and grandmother. She is the author of *RV Chuckles and Chuckholes: the Confessions of Happy Campers,* several magazine articles and a historical novel, *A Place in the Promised Land.* Available at Amazon.com.

Jean Nelson: Jean is sixty-six and retired since 1998. She taught elementary school, parent education, adult basic education, and English as a Second Language. She has been married almost forty-five years and they have two sons. At one point they considered living aboard their sailboat but Jean prefers dry sailing.

Carolyn Talbot: Carolyn is a stay-at-home mom with their dogs and cats, while husband John works for Bechtel Construction. On the road since August 2000, they sold their old house in Kansas City, Missouri, and go from project to project, living in a fifth wheel. The plaque on their Carriage says "House of 44 Legs."

Lucille Tillotson: Originally from Connecticut, Lucille has traveled with her husband of thirty-one years, Larry, during his military career, both in the United States and overseas. Currently living in Alabama, she looks forward to hitting the road in January 2004 as she and Larry take an early retirement and travel full-time along with Shelley, their exuberant St. Bernard.

Linda Willard: Linda, sixty, lives in North Carolina and loves RVing with her husband in their Bounder motorhome for six months a year. Two years ago she also bought a 16-foot Toyota Mini and set out solo on an 8000-mile odyssey to see the western states and Canada. It was a great learning experience, filled with difficulties and unlikely solutions — but always fun.

## EXIT RAMP WRITERS

*These writers contributed their choice tidbits for the Exit Ramps.*

| | |
|---|---|
| JA | Joanne Alexakis |
| NA | Nan Amann |
| SB | Stephanie Bernhagen |
| SBanks | Sally Banks |
| BC | Barbara Cormack |
| CC | Cindy Cook |
| MC | Mary Campbell |
| DE | Donna Ellis |
| AF | Ardith Fenton |
| LE | Lainie Epstein |
| SE | Samantha Eppes |
| JL | Janice Lasko |
| DS | Donna Sauter |
| MS | Mary Schaal |
| CT | Cathi Tessier |
| DW | DeAnna White |
| JW | Janet R. Wilder |

# Index of Contributors

# Pine Country Publishing

ALSO AVAILABLE:

*Support Your RV Lifestyle! An Insider's Guide to Working on the Road, 2nd ed.* By Jaimie Hall. 400 pages. $19.95

*You Shoulda Listened to Your Mother: 36 Timeless Success Tips for Working Women* By Alice Zyetz. 430 pages. $11.95

*The Woman's Guide to Solo RVing.* By Jaimie Hall and Alice Zyetz. In CD ($13.95) or eBook format ($12.95).

*Taking the Mystery out of Retiring to an RV.* By Alice Zyetz. In CD ($10.95) and eBook format ($9.95)

*Taking the Mystery out of RV Writing.* By Jaimie Hall and Alice Zyetz. In CD ($13.95) and eBook format ($12.95)

"RV Lifestyles," the semimonthly electronic newsletter. Subscribe by sending an e-mail to RVlifestyle-subscribe@listbase.net. Or send an e-mail to Jaimie Hall.

———————————

VISIT RV HOMETOWN.COM FOR PRACTICAL INFORMATION ON THE RV LIFESTYLE AND MORE PRODUCTS AT

WWW.RVHOMETOWN.COM

The authors would enjoy hearing from you and invite queries about their books and RV lifestyle questions. Contact them at:
Jaimie Hall is CalamityJaimie@hughes.net
Alice Zyetz is YouShoulda@aol.com

Also visit us at HTTP://www.RVTravelingTales.com

# Order Form

For fax orders: 561/892-2837. Send a copy of this form.

E-mail orders: CalamityJaimie@hughes.net

Postal orders: Pine Country Publishing, 127 Rainbow Dr., #2780, Livingston, TX 77399-1027

On-line credit card orders: HTTP://WWW.RVHOMETOWN.COM

### *RV Traveling Tales*
### *Women's Journeys on the Open Road*
at $14.95 (U.S. funds) per copy

Name: _____

Address: _____

City: _____

State and zip code: _____

Number of books: _____ @ $14.95 U.S. =          $_____

Media rate shipping and handling: $2.50, additional
copies $1.00 each                                                      $_____

Priority Mail shipping and handling: each $4.75          $_____

Texas residents add sales tax: 8.25%                          $_____

Total enclosed:                                                         $_____


Make checks payable to: Pine Country Publishing

For Visa, Mastercard or Discover orders, complete the following:

Name as it appears on your card: _____

Card Number _____ Exp. date_____

Check digit on back. (credit card number plus 3 digits in italics on signature line) Last 3 digits are _____

Signature _____

E-mail or phone number: _____

CPSIA information can be obtained at www.ICGtesting.com
Printed in the USA
BVOW012132011111

274850BV00009B/1/A